Nathan Haselbauer's books include the bestselling
The Mammoth Book of Sudoku and
The Mammoth Book of IQ Puzzles. A second volume,
The Mammoth Book of New IQ Puzzles, is being published
in 2010. He is the founder and President of the
International High IQ Society, the second
largest IQ society in the world.

THE MAMMOTH BOOK OF

QUICK PUZZLES

Introduced by Nathan Haselbauer

ROBINSON   RUNNING PRESS
PHILADELPHIA · LONDON

Constable & Robinson Ltd
3 The Lanchesters
162 Fulham Palace Road
London W6 9ER
www.constablerobinson.com

First published in the UK by Robinson,
an imprint of Constable & Robinson, 2009

A copy of the British Library Cataloguing in Publication
Data is available from the British Library

UK ISBN 978-1-84901-059-7

1 3 5 7 9 10 8 6 4 2

First published in the United States in 2009 by Running Press Book Publishers
All rights reserved under the Pan-American and International Copyright Conventions

9   8   7   6   5   4   3   2   1
Digit on the right indicates the number of this printing

US Library of Congress number: 2008944140
US ISBN 978-0-76243-782-5

Running Press Book Publishers
2300 Chestnut Street
Philadelphia, PA 19103-4371

Visit us on the web!
www.runningpress.com

Puzzle compilation, typesetting and design by: Puzzle Press Ltd
www.puzzlepress.co.uk

Printed and bound in the EU

Contents

INTRODUCTION

The *Mammoth Book of Quick Puzzles* is an equally quick-fire follow-up to the bestselling *Mammoth Book of Fast Puzzles*. Keeping your brain active keeps it healthy and razor-sharp, and recreational puzzles can play a big part in keeping your brain active.

In addition, there is compelling scientific evidence to show that solving a number of different puzzles during a short space of time rather than sticking with a single puzzle is a better way to activate most parts of your brain. To benefit from this effect the puzzles don't have to be that hard; in fact, solving straightforward puzzles rapidly, one after the other, has been shown to be the most effective way of all to keep our brains fit.

This second volume of speed puzzles offers the perfect workout for your brain with challenges ranging from math and logic problems to word games. All the puzzles are straightforward to understand and none of them requires any advanced mathematical knowledge. Most importantly for keeping your brain in shape, it is possible to solve every puzzle in a short space of time.

It is important to note that these "quick" puzzles are *not* the kind of puzzles found at international speed-solving competitions, where contestants have to solve a series of difficult puzzles in the shortest possible time. There is no race here against other contestants or the clock, just an opportunity to exercise your whole brain to keep it at peak fitness.

The puzzles in this collection are designed to distract, not drive you to distraction. Collectively they are perfect stress-busters, the ideal way to relax. And there are few things to beat the feeling of satisfaction of moving swiftly and surely from one solution to another.

Enjoy the puzzles!

Nathan Haselbauer

1

Countries Wordsearch

```
Y K I B N G R E E C E
S D A U G A R A C I N
I C N U M I L B T M V
N A I A T V G A A E R
G E N R L B B C N X J
A A E G D I E E T I L
P A G L R D Z N T C I
O B B I O U A A X O B
R B K N E D L P W B Y
E B I L U Y V B D S A
M A A S Y T M A L T A
```

ERITREA	MEXICO
GREECE	NICARAGUA
ITALY	PANAMA
KIRIBATI	SINGAPORE
LIBYA	SUDAN
MACEDONIA	SWAZILAND
MALTA	VENEZUELA

Sequence Conundrum

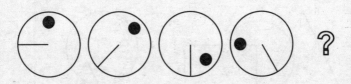

Which one of the lettered alternatives continues the sequence above?

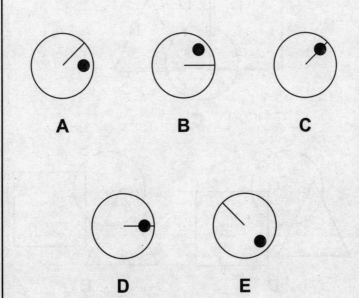

A   B   C

D   E

Odd One Out

Which is the odd one out – and why?

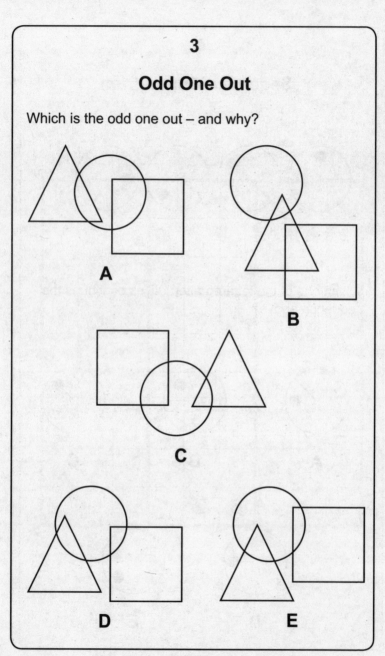

A

B

C

D

E

4

Sudoku

	5			7	3	6		8
	1	2			4			
8					6		5	4
7			4			8	9	
		1	9		5	3		
	4	8			1			2
3	9		5					6
			3			9	7	
5		7	6	2			1	

Wordfit

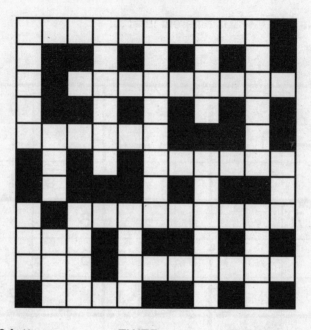

3 letters
ADD
DIE
DRY
HEX
IRE
YES

4 letters
EASY
ECHO
ESPY

EWER
KEYS

5 letters
CADET

6 letters
CRANNY
HOCKEY
SORROW
THRIVE
THROBS

7 letters
SPANIEL

8 letter
STARSHIP

9 letters
KEEPSAKES
TREACHERY

10 letters
CONSISTENT

Spot the Difference

Which of these is different from the rest – and how?

1

2

3

4

5

6

Character Assignation

Fill in the Across clues in this crossword in the normal way. Then read down the diagonal line of eight squares, to reveal:
A character created by J M Barrie (two words).

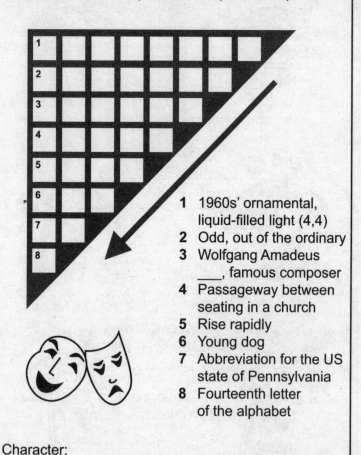

1 1960s' ornamental, liquid-filled light (4,4)
2 Odd, out of the ordinary
3 Wolfgang Amadeus ___, famous composer
4 Passageway between seating in a church
5 Rise rapidly
6 Young dog
7 Abbreviation for the US state of Pennsylvania
8 Fourteenth letter of the alphabet

Character: __ __ __ __ __ __ __ __

8

Pyracross

Solve the clues on each level of the pyramid and reveal the word in the central column of bricks, a clue for which is: Republic in north-west Africa.

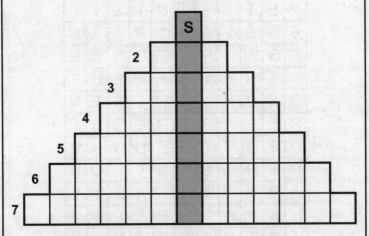

2 Female bird

3 Capital of Belarus

4 Country between Morocco and Tunisia

5 South American region between the Andes and the South Atlantic

6 Largest city in Minnesota

7 Performer who projects his or her voice into a dummy

HIDDEN WORD: _____

Do It Yourself!

The listed words all appear in this crossword – you just need to blank out the unwanted squares…

P	E	T	E	P	I	D	I	S	I	P
E	G	O	V	A	N	I	P	C	A	R
E	S	W	O	R	K	F	O	R	C	E
P	A	N	E	T	A	F	F	E	D	E
O	X	E	N	I	N	E	T	E	E	N
S	L	R	A	C	E	R	E	D	C	A
D	E	S	T	I	N	E	D	O	H	B
R	S	H	I	P	E	N	T	R	O	D
A	V	A	L	A	N	C	H	E	T	E
M	A	P	S	T	R	E	E	L	E	A
A	C	E	S	E	S	S	A	Y	A	F

ACE	EGO	RELY
AVALANCHE	ESSAY	ROD
AXLE	LEA	SCREE
DEAF	NINETEEN	SHAPE
DESTINED	PAN	SIP
DIFFERENCES	PARTICIPATE	TEPID
DRAMA	PEEP	TOWN
ECHO	PREEN	WORKFORCE

Letters Crossword

Each clue consists of letters in alphabetical order. Rearrange these to form words, then fill the grid.

Across
  1 AADIORRST (9)
  6 AEMT (4)
  8 BRRU (4)
  10 ABEKS (5)
  12 EIL (3)
  13 NRU (3)
  14 ADGMO (5)
  17 EENV (4)
  18 AELO (4)
  20 EEIMMOSST (9)

Down
  2 AEP (3)
  3 AIOT (4)
  4 BETU (4)
  5 AEGNRST (7)
  6 EILLMRS (7)
  7 ABDEI (5)
  9 ALSUU (5)
  11 EGK (3)
  15 CENO (4)
  16 AGIM (4)
  19 DEO (3)

11

Around the Clock

Travel around the clock, one hour at a time, making twelve words all ending with the central letter. The letters to be placed in the empty squares are to be found in the segment clockwise of the number to be filled. We've completed one already, in order to get you off to a timely start…

Now take the central letter of every even-numbered word and rearrange these to form another, meaning: Characteristic to be considered.

____ ____ ____ ____ ____ ____

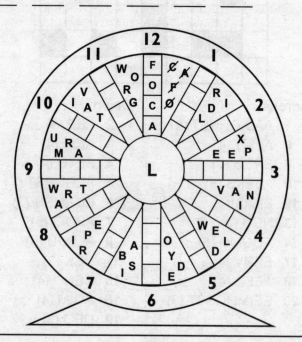

12

Around the Block

You won't need a starting block to get you under way, because it isn't a race! Just arrange the six-letter solutions to the clues into the six blocks around each clue number.

Write the answers in a clockwise or anticlockwise direction and you'll find that the last answer fits into the first; the main problem will be to decide in which square to put the first letter of each word…

1 Paradise
2 Brutal, barbaric
3 Small carnivore which lends its name to a sneaky person
4 Sharp, shrewd
5 Becomes stretched or taut
6 Dairy food

13

Roundword

Write the answer to each clue into the grid, working in a clockwise direction.

Every solution overlaps the next by either one, two, or three letters and each solution starts in its numbered section.

The solution to the final clue ends with the letter in the first square.

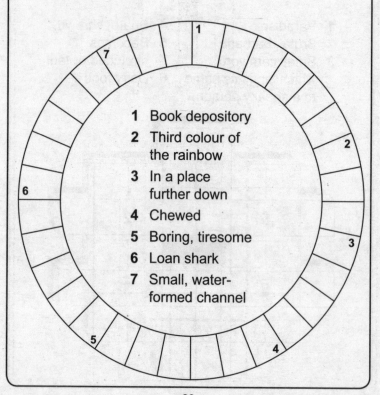

1 Book depository
2 Third colour of the rainbow
3 In a place further down
4 Chewed
5 Boring, tiresome
6 Loan shark
7 Small, water-formed channel

14

Square Filler

The clues list the groups of adjacent blacked-out squares for each row and column, as you can see in this example:

2 3						
1 2						
1 1 1						
1 4						
5						
1 1						
	1 3	2 1	3	5	2 2	1 2 1

Any adjacent blacked-out squares must have at least one white square between them and the next set of adjacent blacked-out squares.

Just follow the clues to fill in each row and column.

3 2						
1 4						
1 2						
6						
1 1 1						
3 2						
	2 3	1 2 1	2 1 1	4	4 1	2 3

15

Dice Section

Printed onto every one of the six numbered dice are six letters (one per side), which can be rearranged to form the answer to each clue; however, some sides are invisible to you. Use the clues and write every answer into the grid. When correctly filled, the letters in the shaded squares, reading in the order 1 to 6, will spell out the name of a cartoon character.

1 Grassy Argentinian plain

2 Small room or wardrobe

3 Idiotic

4 Refrigerator

5 Conformed

6 Capital of Austria

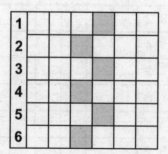

16

Pyramid Plus

Every brick in this pyramid contains a number which is the sum of the two numbers below it, so that F = A + B, etc.

Just work out the missing numbers!

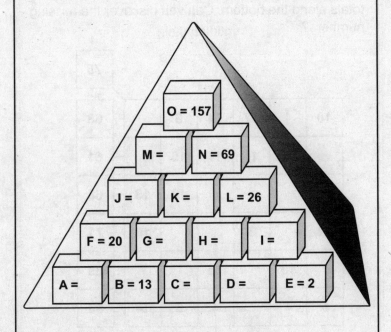

O = 157

M =   N = 69

J =   K =   L = 26

F = 20   G =   H =   I =

A =   B = 13   C =   D =   E = 2

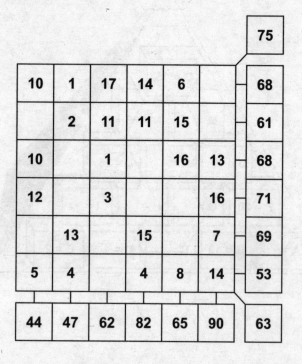

17

Total Concentration

The blank squares below should be filled with whole numbers between 1 and 20 inclusive, any of which may occur more than once, or not at all.

The numbers in every horizontal row add up to the totals on the right, as do the two long diagonal lines; whilst those in every vertical column add up to the totals along the bottom. Can you discover the missing numbers?

						Totals
						75
10	1	17	14	6		68
	2	11	11	15		61
10		1		16	13	68
12		3			16	71
	13		15		7	69
5	4		4	8	14	53
44	47	62	82	65	90	63

18

Hexagony

Can you place the hexagons into the grid, so that where any hexagon touches another along a straight line, the contents of both triangles are the same? No rotation of any hexagon is allowed!

19

Number Fit

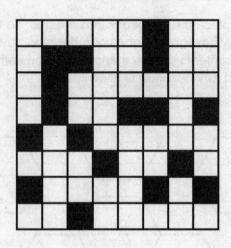

2 digits	3 digits	5 digits
19	232	15902
20	518	37691
26	816	42778
29		59700
50		63838
54		
55		
67	**4 digits**	**6 digits**
71	2954	166478
90	5242	
91	6258	
99	7320	

20

Sudoku

1					4		9	8
	2		8		5			1
7	4			9	3			
		7		3	8	6		
8		5				7		4
		3	4	7		9		
			6	4			2	7
6			3		1		4	
9	8		2					3

Box Clever

When the box below is folded to form a cube, just one of the five options (A, B, C, D, or E) can be produced. Which?

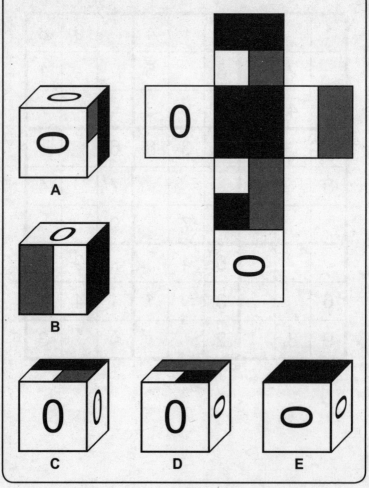

A

B

C

D

E

22

Sequence Conundrum

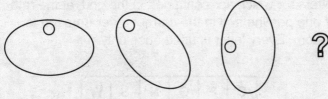

Which one of the lettered alternatives continues the sequence above?

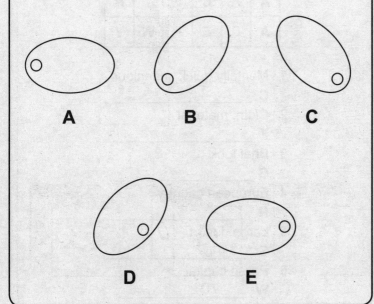

23

Downwords

The solutions to the clues are all six-letter words, the letters for which are contained in the grid, at the rate of one per line and in the correct order from top to bottom. Every letter is used once only.

C	F	G	N	S	W
A	A	A	L	L	O
A	B	E	H	R	R
A	N	R	S	V	W
A	A	C	E	I	R
A	C	E	R	W	Y

1 Mentally quick, ingenious

C _____

2 Cloth, material

F _____

3 Brief look

G _____

4 European country

N _____

5 Large desert

S _____

6 Polish capital

W _____

24

Sum Circle

Fill the three empty circles with the symbols +, −, and x in some order to make a sum which totals the number in the centre.

Each symbol must be used once and calculations are made in the direction of travel (clockwise).

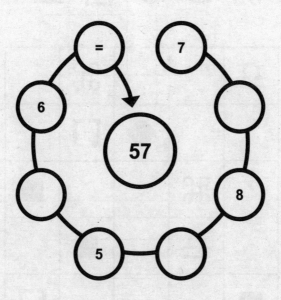

25

Shape Up

Each row and column of this grid should be filled with one of five different symbols, so that all five appear in that row or column.

Some are already in place – can you complete the grid?

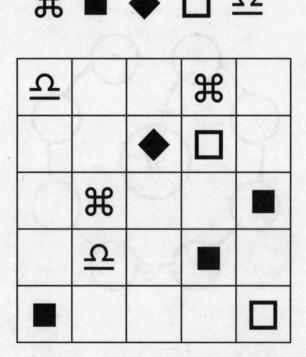

26

Eliminator

Every oval shape in this diagram contains a different letter of the alphabet from A to K inclusive. Use the clues to determine their locations. Reference in the clues to "due" means in any location along the same horizontal or vertical line.

1 B is due north of E, which is due east of C.

2 C is next to and south of K, which is next to and west of F.

3 F is due south of A, but due north of D.

4 G is due east of I, which is due east of H.

5 H is further north than B.

6 J is further north than D.

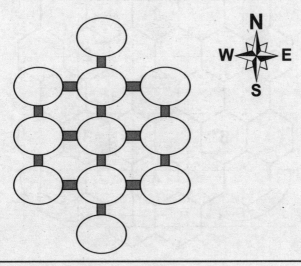

Hexafit

Can you place these six words into the hexagons? To fit them all in, some will have to be entered clockwise and others anticlockwise around the numbers.

Two letters have been placed already, which should give you a good start!

COUGAR   FLUENT   GUILTY

LIFTED   RAILED   STYLUS

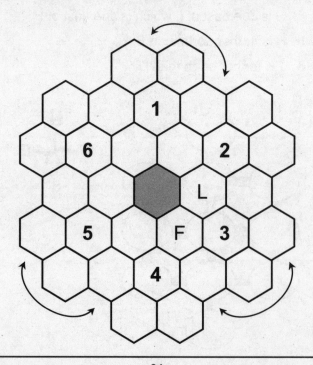

28

Stamp It Out!

Can you pair each of the stamps with its correct print?

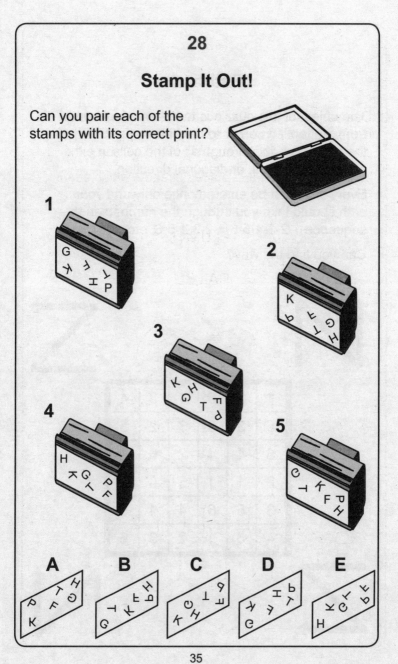

Pathfinder

The object of this puzzle is to trace a single path from the top left corner to the bottom right corner of the grid, travelling through all of the cells in either a horizontal, vertical, or diagonal direction.

Every cell must be entered once only and your path should take you through the numbers in the sequence 1-2-3-4-5-6-1-2-3-4-5-6, etc.

Can you find the way?

1	2	6	1	3	4
5	3	5	3	2	5
6	4	4	2	6	1
2	1	1	5	3	2
3	5	6	4	4	5
4	6	1	2	3	6

30

Memory Game

Study the picture below for 30 seconds and then turn to page 237.

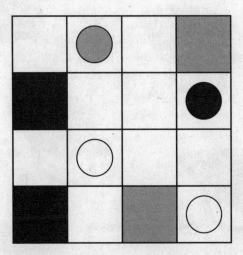

This part of the test relates to the puzzle on page 287. Which of the following have you just seen?

1   2   3

Shadows

Which of the shadows below is
that of the kettle shown here?

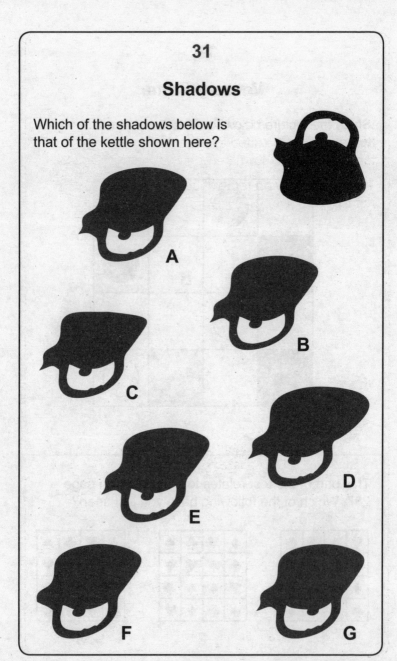

A

B

C

E

D

F

G

32

Jigsaw Puzzle

Which four shapes (two black and two white) can be fitted together to form the shape shown here?

The pieces may be rotated, but not flipped over.

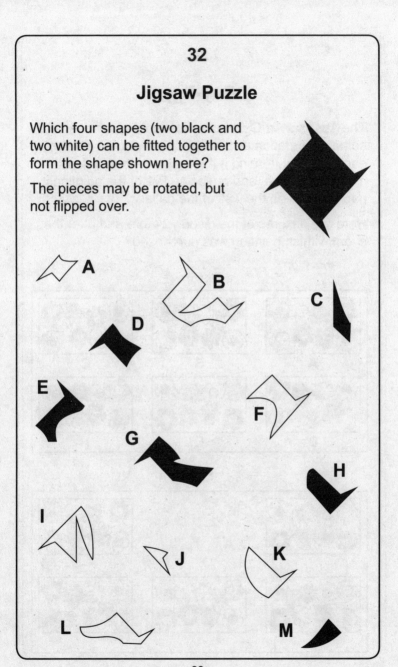

A

B

C

D

E

F

G

H

I

J

K

L

M

33

Buy-Buy

The Abstract Art Gallery has just sold a painting, after some deliberation by the customer, who took down each painting, turning it this way and that, before making a choice, and replacing five of the paintings haphazardly on the wall of the gallery.

Here are pictures of the display before and after the event. Which painting was purchased?

Before

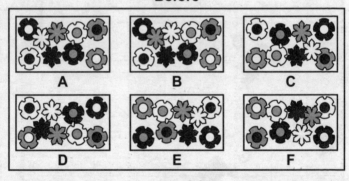

After

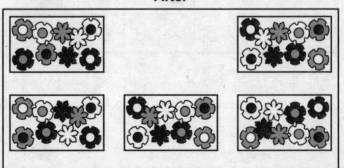

34

Sudoku

		4	9	1	5	6		
7		5	8			4		3
	9		7					5
	3		6					9
6		1				2		8
5					7		1	
1					8		6	
2		8			3	9		4
		7	5	2	6	8		

Word Ladder

Change one letter at a time (but not the position of any letter) to make a new word – and move from the word at the top of the ladder to the word at the bottom, using the exact number of rungs provided.

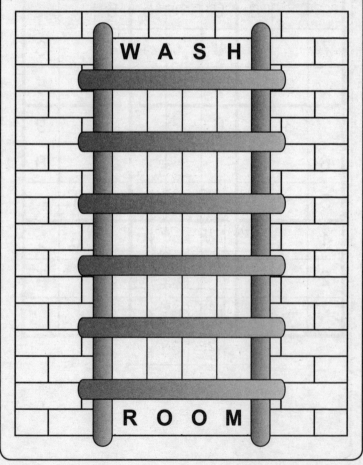

W A S H

R O O M

36

Treasure Hunt

The chart below gives directions to a hidden treasure behind the central black square in the grid.

Move the indicated number of spaces north, south, east, and west (e.g., 4N would mean four squares north) stopping at each square once only to arrive there.

At which square should you start?

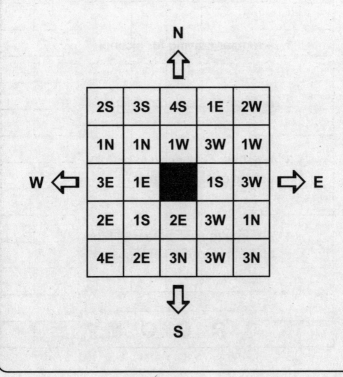

Wordpower

Which one of the four alternatives is the correct definition of the word shown below?

DIPSOMANIA

1 A regular craving for alcohol

2 An urge to steal from friends

3 A pathological need to acquire educational certificates

4 An urge to associate with high officials in foreign embassies

38

Maze

Can you trace your way through this maze, without taking your pencil from the paper?

39

Wordwheel

How many words of three or more letters can you make from those in the wheel, without using plurals, abbreviations, or proper nouns in just three minutes?

The central letter must appear once in every word and no letter in a section of the wheel may be used more than once.

There is at least one nine-letter word in the wheel.

Nine-letter word(s):

Tile Twister

Place the eight tiles into the puzzle grid so that all adjacent numbers on each tile match up. Any tile may be rotated, but none may be flipped over.

2	1
4	3

2	3
3	4

1	3
1	2

4	3
2	1

1	1
3	2

3	3
4	1

3	3
3	2

1	3
3	1

				4	2
				2	3

Bermuda Triangle

Travel through the "Bermuda Triangle" by visiting one room at a time to collect a letter from each. You can enter the outside passageway as often as you like, but can only visit each room once.

When you've completed your tour, the 15 letters (in order) will spell out a word.

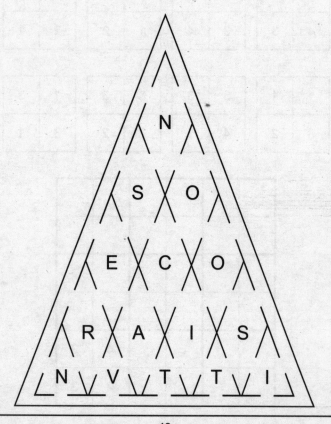

42

Shape Spotter

Which is the only shape to appear twice in the box below? You'll need a keen eye for this one, as some shapes overlap others!

Link Words

Fit different words into the central columns of the grid, so that each one links up with the words to either side, for example: table – lamp – shade.

When finished, read down the letters in the shaded squares to reveal another word, solving the clue below the grid.

SAW					**BOWL**
GOOD					**PAPER**
SHAM					**BOTTOM**
WIND					**YARD**
BIRTHDAY					**WALK**
MOUNTAIN					**AWAY**
BRANDING					**AGE**
DUCK					**LOAD**

Clue: Type of turtle

Word: _____

44

Half and Half

Pair off these groups of three letters to make eight units of currency (past and present), each comprising six letters.

KKA   FOR   SHE   DEN

KEL   DOL   BLE   ESC

UDO   ETA   MAR   PES

GUL   ROU   INT   LAR

_____   _____

_____   _____

_____   _____

_____   _____

45

Couplets

The picture is of a central circle surrounded by shapes, linked to form six sets of three shapes apiece. Can you complete the puzzle by placing each of the two-letter groups below, one per shape, so that every set of three (the central circle, plus the two matching shapes diagonally opposite one another) forms a six-letter word? Whichever pair of letters you place in the central circle will appear in the middle of every word.

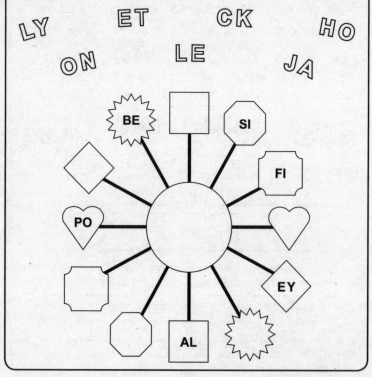

LY   ET   CK   HO

ON   LE   JA

46

Keyword

On the face of it, this puzzle seems straightforward. Simply fill in the letters missing from words 1-8 and enter them into the numbered boxes, to reveal a hidden keyword.

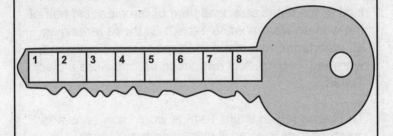

	1	2	3	4	5	6	7	8

1 C __ O S E __ N

2 __ I G H __ T __ Y

3 P R __ N C __ E

4 D A N C E __

5 N E A R __ __ Y

6 B L __ U S E

7 Z E A L __ __ T

8 E __ B E R __ S

Fractional Process

Sixteen cyclists took part in a ten-mile cross-country race. One quarter were teenage riders and the remainder was made up of equal numbers of adult men and women.

Half of the teenagers, one third of the men and half of the women wore a white T-shirt. Of those remaining, one teenager, half of the men, and all of the women wore red T-shirts. Any remaining person wore a black T-shirt.

The teenagers in white T-shirts wore blue jeans and any teenager in a red T-shirt wore black jeans. All the men and one of the women in white T-shirts wore black jeans. Two men in red T-shirts and two women in white T-shirts wore blue jeans. Any remaining person wore green jeans.

All the teenagers in a white/blue combination, half the men in white/black, half the men in red/blue, one woman in white/black, and two thirds of the women in red T-shirts pulled out of the race at some point.

How many people completed the race?

48

Cut Out

Can you pair up shapes with the squares from which they were cut? Some may have been flipped over.

1

2

3

4

5

6

A

B

C

D

E

F

49

In at the Count

Precisely how many kites are in this picture?

Follow the Thread

These fishing lines have become tangled. Can you sort out which fish has been caught by each angler?

51

Playing Cards Wordsearch

```
N N H Z A D E V V I M
N J E M S T O C K Y I
M B M E P I R X R S D
R E R F U H W A E P G
E E R H T Q S S C I S
K E U C H R E B U H R
O G Q C E J A U E C O
J S E V E N K L D J Y
K Y D R K L I C X O A
P A Q E O K N A V E L
R O R G S I G S W L P
```

ADVERSARY	KING
BANKER	KNAVE
CHIPS	QUEEN
CLUBS	ROYAL
DEUCE	SEVEN
EUCHRE	STOCK
JOKER	THREE

Sequence Conundrum

Which one of the lettered alternatives continues the sequence above?

A

B

C

D

E

53

Odd One Out

Which is the odd one out – and why?

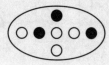

A

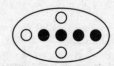

B

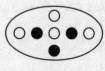

C

D

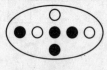

E

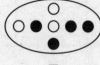

F

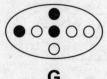

G

Sudoku

4				1		8	5	6
6			9	7	8			
3			4		5			
		6	1		3		9	
5		7				1		2
	3		5		7	6		
			2		9			1
			8	4	6			9
9	2	8		3				4

Wordfit

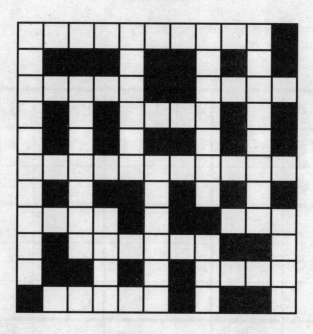

3 letters
JET
RAW

4 letters
ACRE
CLEF
FETA
INTO
PAVE
TREE

5 letters
TRAMP
WRAPS

6 letters
EMPIRE
NAPLES
SELLER

7 letters
AVENUES
OPPOSED

8 letters
DIVORCEE

10 letters
MOTHERHOOD
MOTORCYCLE

11 letters
CONVENIENCE

Spot the Difference

Which of these is different from the rest – and how?

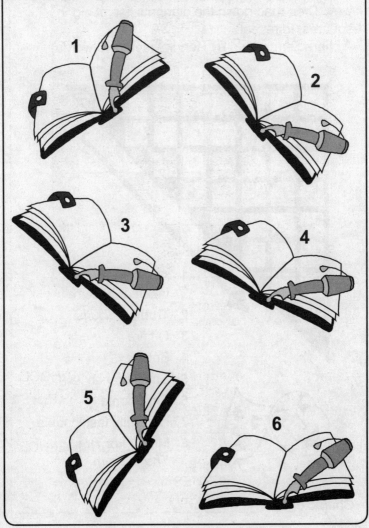

57

Character Assignation

Fill in the Across clues in this crossword in the normal way. Then read down the diagonal line of eight squares, to reveal:
A character created by Henrik Ibsen (two words).

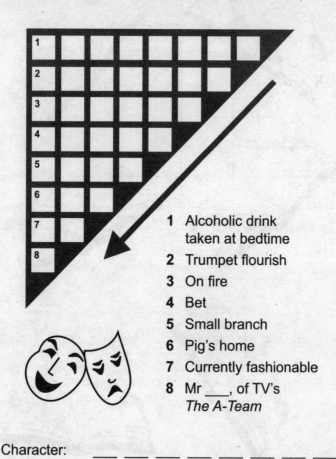

1 Alcoholic drink taken at bedtime
2 Trumpet flourish
3 On fire
4 Bet
5 Small branch
6 Pig's home
7 Currently fashionable
8 Mr ___, of TV's *The A-Team*

Character: __ __ __ __ __ __ __ __

58

Pyracross

Solve the clues on each level of the pyramid and reveal the word in the central column of bricks, a clue for which is: Philistine warrior slain by David.

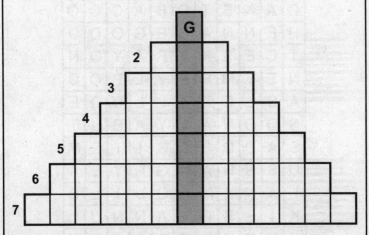

2 Constricting snake

3 Book of maps

4 Country, capital Windhoek

5 Nut with an edible green kernel

6 Sign of the zodiac

7 US state, capital Boston

HIDDEN WORD: _____

59

Do It Yourself!

The listed words all appear in this crossword – you just need to blank out the unwanted squares…

C	A	K	E	T	O	B	A	C	C	O
H	E	N	N	A	B	E	G	O	D	U
I	C	E	S	K	Y	R	A	Y	O	N
N	E	E	M	E	R	Y	L	P	O	C
A	B	L	E	B	A	L	L	U	D	E
S	O	O	N	A	V	Y	A	B	U	T
S	A	D	D	L	E	S	I	T	E	M
U	S	E	R	A	N	G	R	Y	E	A
L	A	N	K	Y	A	O	U	I	L	P
K	I	S	S	E	V	A	N	N	U	L
S	N	E	E	R	E	D	I	G	L	E

ABLE	EMERY	MEND
ALLUDE	GOAD	OUNCE
ANGRY	HENNA	RAVEN
ANNUL	ITEM	RAYON
BERYL	KNEEL	SADDLE
BOA	LAIR	SNEERED
CHINA	LANKY	SULKS
COYPU	LAYER	TAKE
DENSE	MAPLE	TOBACCO
DUE		TYING

Letters Crossword

Each clue consists of letters in alphabetical order. Rearrange these to form words, then fill the grid.

Across

1 IQSTU (5)
6 INTUY (5)
7 ABIRR (5)
9 AEELPR (6)
12 CEIP (4)
14 EELS (4)
15 AEHLLT (6)
17 ERTTU (5)
18 HEORT (5)
19 AEGNT (5)

Down

2 EINPRU (6)
3 ERSU (4)
4 EILPX (5)
5 CCELY (5)
8 ACHR (4)
10 ELPT (4)
11 AENRST (6)
12 BELOW (5)
13 CHITY (5)
16 AARU (4)

Around the Clock

Travel around the clock, one hour at a time, making twelve words all ending with the central letter. The letters to be placed in the empty squares are to be found in the segment clockwise of the number to be filled. We've completed one already, in order to get you off to a timely start…

Now take the central letter of every even-numbered word and rearrange these to form another, meaning: Physical power.

___ ___ ___ ___ ___ ___

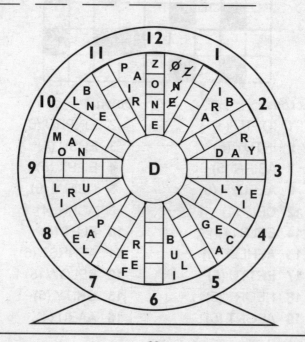

62

Around the Block

You won't need a starting block to get you under way, because it isn't a race! Just arrange the six-letter solutions to the clues into the six blocks around each clue number.

Write the answers in a clockwise or anticlockwise direction and you'll find that the last answer fits into the first; the main problem will be to decide in which square to put the first letter of each word…

1 Country, capital Oslo
2 Study of plants
3 Nonentity

4 Short period of time
5 Son of a sovereign
6 Gradually decreasing, ebbing

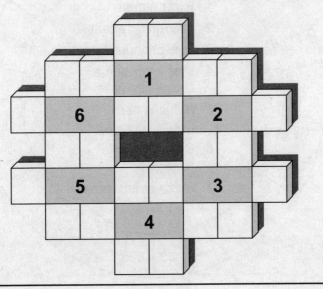

63

Roundword

Write the answer to each clue into the grid, working in a clockwise direction.

Every solution overlaps the next by either one, two, or three letters and each solution starts in its numbered section.

The solution to the final clue ends with the letter in the first square.

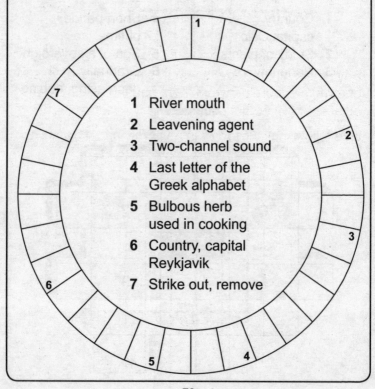

1 River mouth
2 Leavening agent
3 Two-channel sound
4 Last letter of the Greek alphabet
5 Bulbous herb used in cooking
6 Country, capital Reykjavik
7 Strike out, remove

64

Square Filler

The clues list the groups of adjacent blacked-out squares for each row and column, as you can see in this example:

2 3						
1 2						
1 1 1						
1 4						
5						
1 1						
	1 3	2 1	3	5	2 2	1 2 1

Any adjacent blacked-out squares must have at least one white square between them and the next set of adjacent blacked-out squares.

Just follow the clues to fill in each row and column.

6						
4 1						
2 1						
1 4						
2 1						
1 4						
	2 1 1	3	6	2 3	1 1 1	6

65

Dice Section

Printed onto every one of the six numbered dice are six letters (one per side), which can be rearranged to form the answer to each clue; however, some sides are invisible to you. Use the clues and write every answer into the grid. When correctly filled, the letters in the shaded squares, reading in the order 1 to 6, will spell out the name of a comic-book superhero.

1 Increase twofold

2 Divided up

3 Sticky fluid found in flowers

4 Look up to

5 Japanese system of unarmed combat

6 US Sunflower State

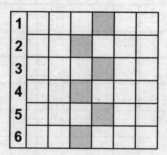

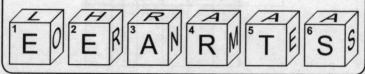

66

Pyramid Plus

Every brick in this pyramid contains a number which is the sum of the two numbers below it, so that F = A + B, etc.

Just work out the missing numbers!

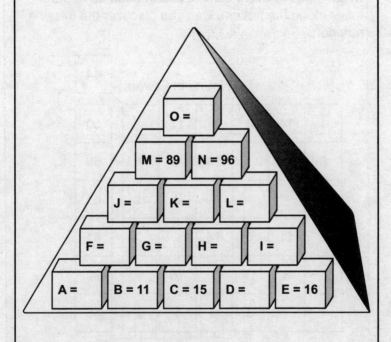

Total Concentration

The blank squares below should be filled with whole numbers between 1 and 20 inclusive, any of which may occur more than once, or not at all.

The numbers in every horizontal row add up to the totals on the right, as do the two long diagonal lines; whilst those in every vertical column add up to the totals along the bottom. Can you discover the missing numbers?

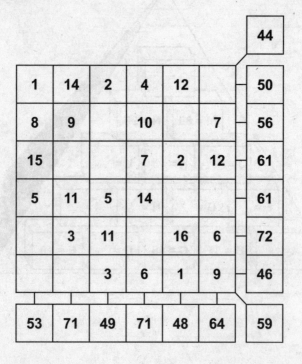

						44
1	14	2	4	12		50
8	9		10		7	56
15			7	2	12	61
5	11	5	14			61
	3	11		16	6	72
		3	6	1	9	46
53	71	49	71	48	64	59

68

Hexagony

Can you place the hexagons into the grid, so that where any hexagon touches another along a straight line, the contents of both triangles are the same? No rotation of any hexagon is allowed!

69

Number Fit

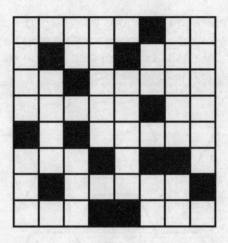

2 digits	3 digits	5 digits
12	370	17235
22	473	23450
30	523	37820
38	684	51356
41	685	60451
44	823	72554
58		74034
88		78482

4 digits	6 digits
2257	200011
8248	

Sudoku

					1			7
	7	6	2	8		1		
1					6	3	4	
	2	9	4			5	8	
8				9				6
	1	5			7	9	3	
	5	7	3					2
		8		1	9	4	7	
4			5					

Box Clever

When the box below is folded to form a cube, just one of the five options (A, B, C, D, or E) can be produced. Which?

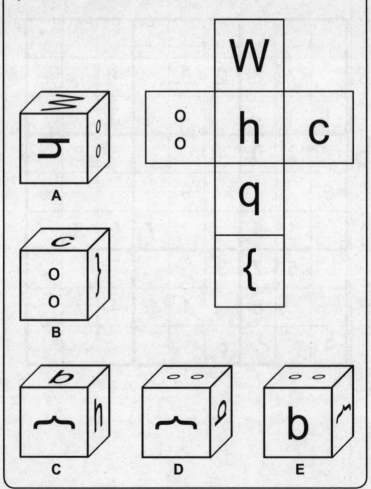

Sequence Conundrum

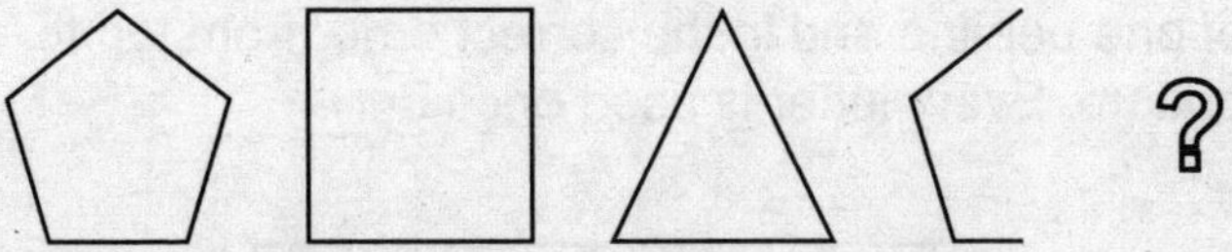

Which one of the lettered alternatives continues the sequence above?

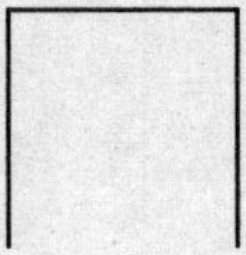

A 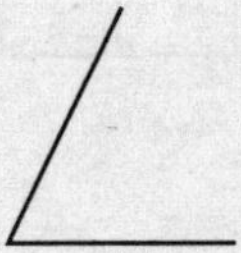 B 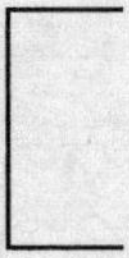 C

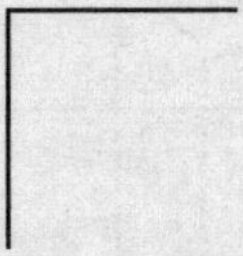

D 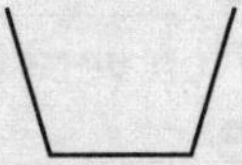 E

Downwords

The solutions to the clues are all six-letter words, the letters for which are contained in the grid, at the rate of one per line and in the correct order from top to bottom. Every letter is used once only.

B	D	K	O	S	W
I	N	O	O	P	S
I	N	P	R	S	Z
D	E	G	I	I	R
C	E	E	H	N	N
G	R	T	T	T	Y

1 Cut in half
B _____

2 Lightly sleeping
D _____

3 Chess piece with a horse's head
K _____

4 "Fish" or "sea" eagle
O _____

5 Run very fast
S _____

6 Amazement
W _____

Sum Circle

Fill the three empty circles with the symbols +, −, and x in some order to make a sum which totals the number in the centre.

Each symbol must be used once and calculations are made in the direction of travel (clockwise).

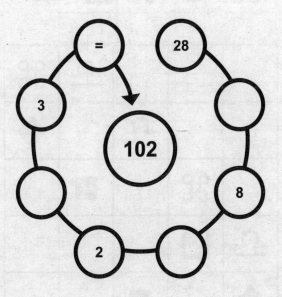

Shape Up

Each row and column of this grid should be filled with one of five different symbols, so that all five appear in that row or column.

Some are already in place – can you complete the grid?

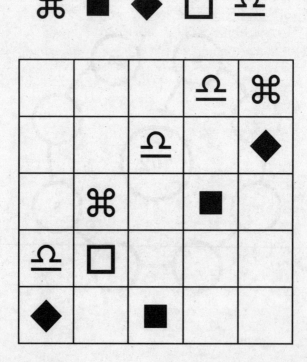

76

Eliminator

Every oval shape in this diagram contains a different letter of the alphabet from A to K inclusive. Use the clues to determine their locations. Reference in the clues to "due" means in any location along the same horizontal or vertical line.

1. A is next to and west of D, which is due south of C.

2. B is next to and west of K, which is next to and north of G.

3. E is next to and south of I, which is next to and west of G.

4. F is further south than H and further west than J.

5. H is further north and further west than C.

6. J is further north than E, but further south than B.

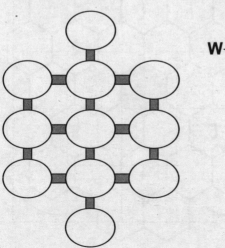

Hexafit

Can you place these six words into the hexagons? To fit them all in, some will have to be entered clockwise and others anticlockwise around the numbers.

Two letters have been placed already, which should give you a good start!

ENAMEL   MARINE   NATURE

RATTLE   REVEAL   RITUAL

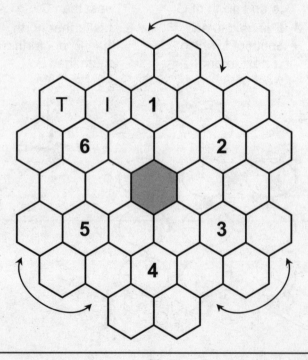

78

Stamp It Out!

Can you pair each of the stamps with its correct print?

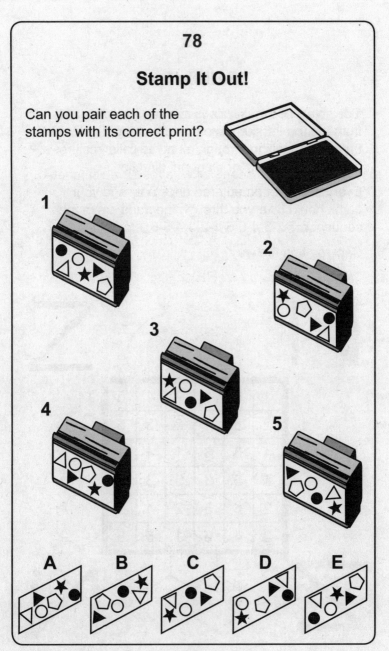

79

Pathfinder

The object of this puzzle is to trace a single path from the top left corner to the bottom right corner of the grid, travelling through all of the cells in either a horizontal, vertical, or diagonal direction.

Every cell must be entered once only and your path should take you through the numbers in the sequence 1-2-3-4-5-6-1-2-3-4-5-6, etc.

Can you find the way?

1	6	1	2	4	5
2	5	4	2	3	6
4	3	3	1	4	1
1	5	6	5	3	2
2	6	5	2	4	3
3	4	6	1	5	6

80

Memory Game

Study the picture below for 30 seconds and then turn to page 287.

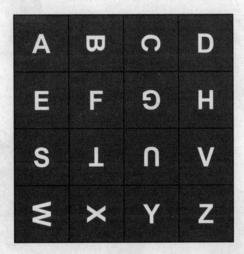

This part of the test relates to the puzzle on page 137. Which of the following have you just seen?

1

2

3

81

Shadows

Which of the shadows below is that of the horse shown here?

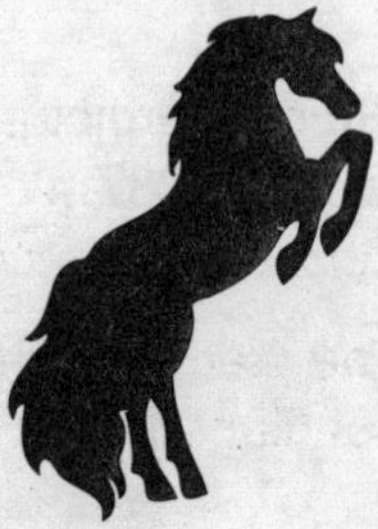

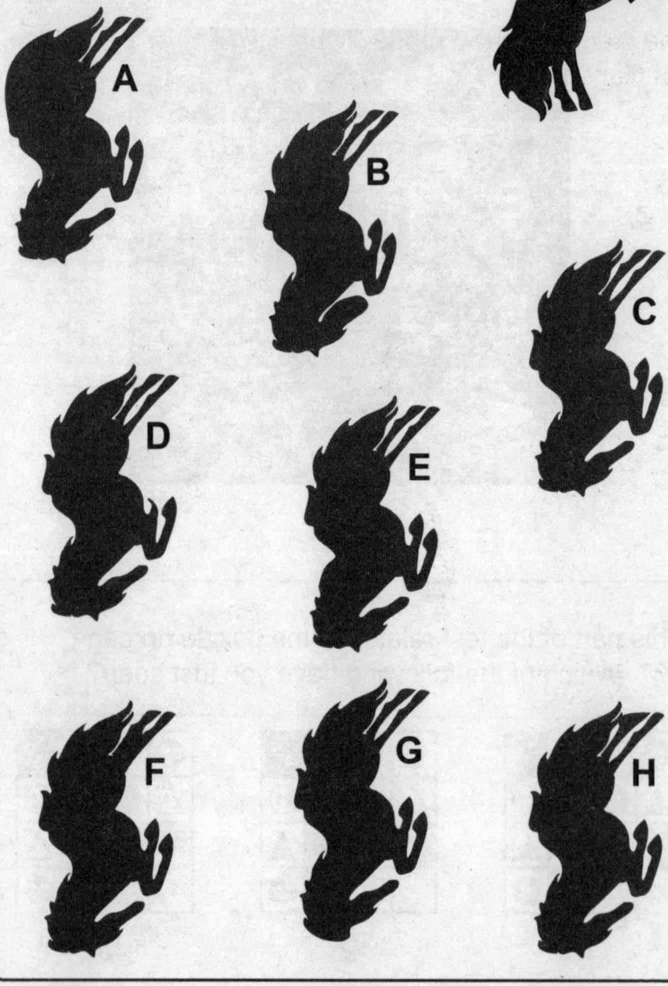

Jigsaw Puzzle

Which four shapes (two black and two white) can be fitted together to form the shape shown here?

The pieces may be rotated, but not flipped over.

A

B

C

D

E

F

G

H

I

J

K

L

M

83

Buy-Buy

The Abstract Art Gallery has just sold a painting, after some deliberation by the customer, who took down each painting, turning it this way and that, before making a choice, and replacing five of the paintings haphazardly on the wall of the gallery.

Here are pictures of the display before and after the event. Which painting was purchased?

Before

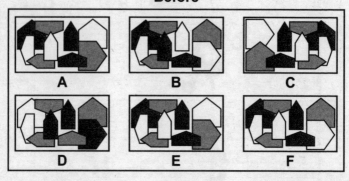

After

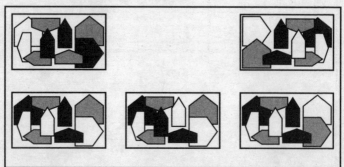

84

Sudoku

2	5				7	4		
	3	6	5	9		7		
	9				8			3
	7			8		1		9
8			7		5			6
3		5		6			4	
5			1				2	
		4		2	9	3	1	
		1	3				7	8

Word Ladder

Change one letter at a time (but not the position of any letter) to make a new word – and move from the word at the top of the ladder to the word at the bottom, using the exact number of rungs provided.

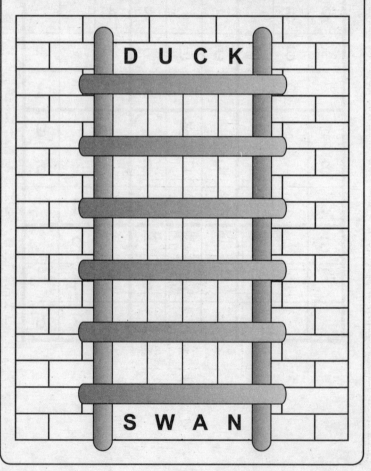

DUCK

SWAN

86

Treasure Hunt

The chart below gives directions to a hidden treasure behind the central black square in the grid.

Move the indicated number of spaces north, south, east, and west (e.g., 4N would mean four squares north) stopping at each square once only to arrive there.

At which square should you start?

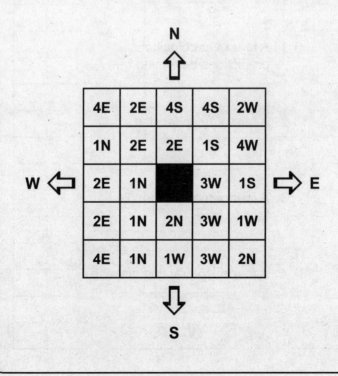

N

4E	2E	4S	4S	2W
1N	2E	2E	1S	4W
2E	1N	■	3W	1S
2E	1N	2N	3W	1W
4E	1N	1W	3W	2N

W ⇐   ⇒ E

S

Wordpower

Which one of the four alternatives is the correct definition of the word shown below?

NOSOPHOBIA

1 A fear of astrological predictions becoming true

2 A fear of hospital staff, especially nurses

3 A fear of meeting people face to face

4 A fear of contracting disease

88

Maze

Can you trace your way through this maze, without taking your pencil from the paper?

Wordwheel

How many words of three or more letters can you make from those in the wheel, without using plurals, abbreviations, or proper nouns in just three minutes?

The central letter must appear once in every word and no letter in a section of the wheel may be used more than once.

There is at least one nine-letter word in the wheel.

Nine-letter word(s):

90

Tile Twister

Place the eight tiles into the puzzle grid so that all adjacent numbers on each tile match up. Any tile may be rotated, but none may be flipped over.

4	2
3	2

1	4
2	3

3	4
2	4

4	2
1	4

2	3
4	2

4	1
2	1

2	1
1	4

2	2
3	1

		4	3		
		1	4		

Bermuda Triangle

Travel through the "Bermuda Triangle" by visiting one room at a time to collect a letter from each. You can enter the outside passageway as often as you like, but can only visit each room once.

When you've completed your tour, the 15 letters (in order) will spell out a word.

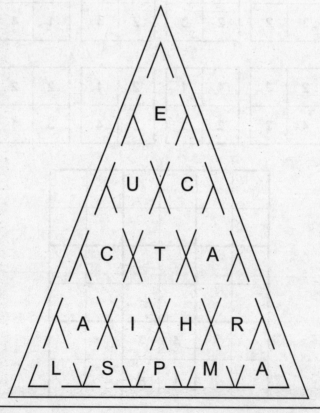

92

Shape Spotter

Which is the only shape to appear twice in the box below? You'll need a keen eye for this one, as some shapes overlap others!

93

Link Words

Fit different words into the central columns of the grid, so that each one links up with the words to either side, for example: table – lamp – shade.

When finished, read down the letters in the shaded squares to reveal another word, solving the clue below the grid.

BACK					ROBE
NAVY					NILE
FOOL'S					MEDAL
FLAG					VAULT
CURTAIN					BOX
EVENING					BOARD
STREET					CRACK
CEDAR					LAND

Clue: Set free

Word: _____

Half and Half

Pair off these groups of three letters to make eight herbs and spices, each comprising six letters.

VES   SOP   GIN   IVE

NEL   LOV   CHI   NUT

END   AGE   MEG   HYS

AGE   FEN   GER   BOR

_____   _____

_____   _____

_____   _____

_____   _____

95

Couplets

The picture is of a central circle surrounded by shapes, linked to form six sets of three shapes apiece. Can you complete the puzzle by placing each of the two-letter groups below, one per shape, so that every set of three (the central circle, plus the two matching shapes diagonally opposite one another) forms a six-letter word? Whichever pair of letters you place in the central circle will appear in the middle of every word.

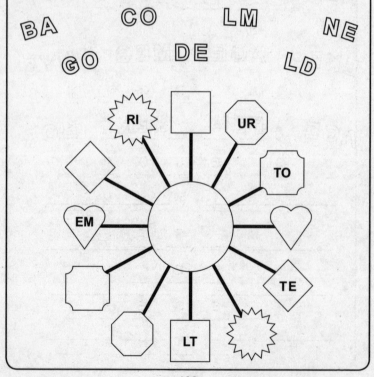

96

Keyword

On the face of it, this puzzle seems straightforward. Simply fill in the letters missing from words 1-8 and enter them into the numbered boxes, to reveal a hidden keyword.

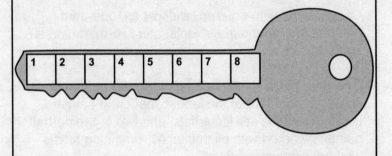

| 1 | 2 | 3 | 4 | 5 | 6 | 7 | 8 |

1 A __ R O A D

2 P A __ P E R

3 __ E S O R T

4 A I M I N __

5 M __ S T E R

6 A V E __ U E

7 __ E S E R T

8 P __ T H O N

Fractional Process

Eighteen amateur artists took part in a painting competition. One half painted a landscape and the remainder was made up of one-third still life subjects and two-thirds portraits of people.

Of the artists who entered landscapes, one-third had painted mountain subjects, and two-thirds forest subjects.

One-third of the landscape painters with mountain subjects, one-third of the landscape/forest painters, two-thirds of the still life artists, and two of the portrait painters worked with oil paints. All remaining artists worked with watercolours.

How many artists worked with watercolours?

98

Cut Out

Can you pair up shapes with the squares from which they were cut? Some may have been flipped over.

1

2

3

4

5

6

A

B

C

D

E

F

In at the Count

Precisely how many balloons are in this picture?

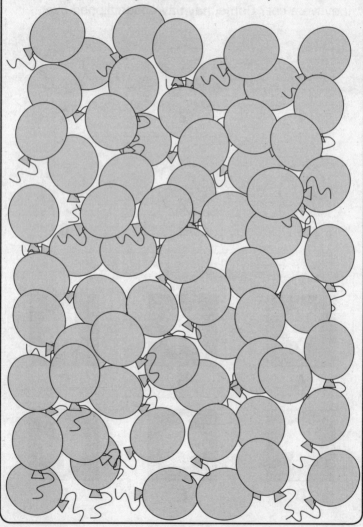

Follow the Thread

These fishing lines have become tangled. Can you sort out which fish has been caught by each angler?

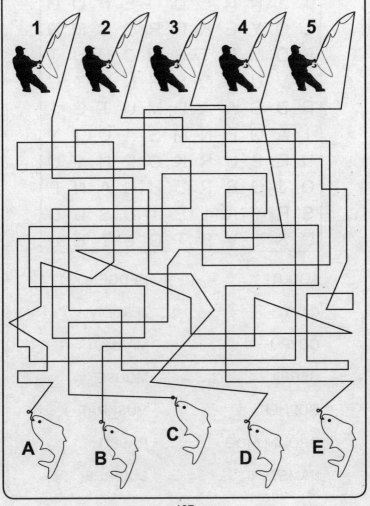

101

Rodents Wordsearch

```
U P Y O C A V O J W Z
T X R H E D G E H O G
L O Y E K D R O G M N
E D M L T B M O U U T
R V U R O S H N M T G
R D G A A D M U T G I
I A G E N M S A O J Y
U E B U R K O P H V Q
Q J O B R B H U A N F
S R Y A I E I C S U D
G S T V R T G L T E U
```

AGOUTI   HEDGEHOG

CAVY   JERBOA

COYPU   MARMOT

GERBIL   MOUSE

GOPHER   MUSKRAT

GROUNDHOG   RABBIT

HAMSTER   SQUIRREL

Sequence Conundrum

Which one of the lettered alternatives continues the sequence above?

A   **B**   **C**

D   **E**

103

Odd One Out

Which is the odd one out – and why?

A

B

C

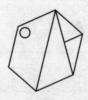

D

E

104

Sudoku

8	3					9		2
	9			7		5		6
				3	1	7	4	
5			6			8		
6	4		3		7		9	5
		2			4			1
	6	9	1	8				
7		5		6			2	
4		1					8	3

105

Wordfit

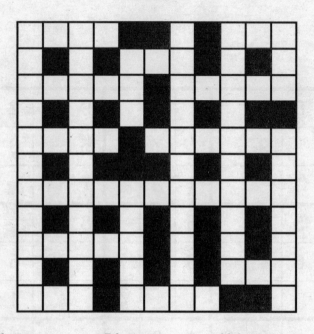

3 letters
FIT
KEG
TAP
THE
WAN
WHY

4 letters
CUBA
LARK
LYNX

5 letters
ICILY
NINTH
ROYAL
SWAMP

6 letters
EIGHTY

7 letters
YIELDED

10 letters
FLASHLIGHT

11 letters
BANKRUPTING
CANDLESTICK
INSPIRATION
SUPERLATIVE

106

Spot the Difference

Which of these is different from the rest – and how?

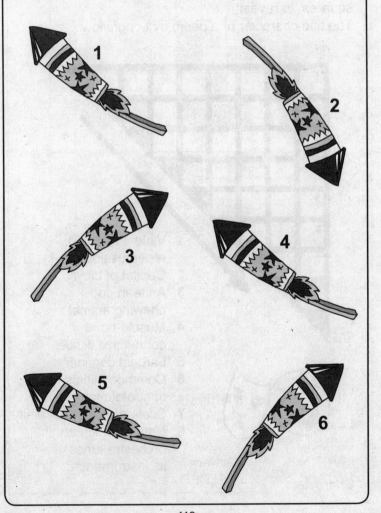

107

Character Assignation

Fill in the Across clues in this crossword in the normal way. Then read down the diagonal line of eight squares, to reveal:
The title character of a poem by Longfellow.

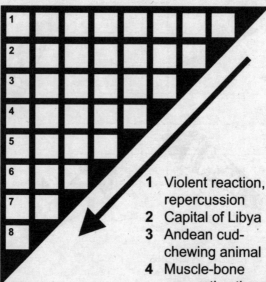

1 Violent reaction, repercussion
2 Capital of Libya
3 Andean cud-chewing animal
4 Muscle-bone connective tissue
5 Largest continent
6 Common initials for trinitrotoluene
7 Scale of acidity-alkalinity
8 Note to which an orchestra tunes its instruments

Character: __ __ __ __ __ __ __ __

108

Pyracross

Solve the clues on each level of the pyramid and reveal the word in the central column of bricks, a clue for which is: Greek mountain.

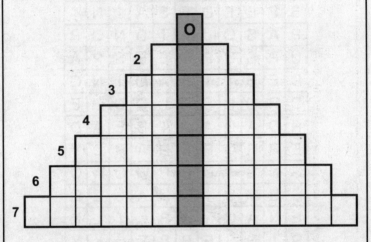

2 Crafty, cunning

3 Country, capital Cairo

4 Sleep

5 Flag signalling system

6 Largest city in New Mexico

7 Postpone or delay needlessly

HIDDEN WORD: _____

109

Do It Yourself!

The listed words all appear in this crossword – you just need to blank out the unwanted squares…

S	P	E	E	D	E	S	A	I	N	T
P	A	S	Q	U	A	T	D	N	O	R
U	P	S	U	R	G	E	E	S	P	A
D	E	B	I	T	E	A	M	I	N	G
D	R	O	P	S	R	L	O	D	G	E
R	O	A	D	A	C	T	B	E	A	D
E	R	R	O	R	L	H	A	R	D	Y
S	N	S	I	D	E	R	W	O	W	O
S	U	M	S	I	N	H	A	L	E	R
E	N	A	O	N	A	B	K	I	L	K
R	I	N	S	E	B	B	E	L	L	Y

ACT	HARDY	SAINT
AWAKE	INHALER	SARDINE
BELLY	INSIDER	SPA
DRESSER	LODGE	SPEED
DROPS	OARSMAN	STEALTH
DWELL	PAPER	SUM
EQUIP	RINSE	TRAGEDY
ERROR		UPSURGE

116

110

Letters Crossword

Each clue consists of letters in alphabetical order.
Rearrange these to form words, then fill the grid.

Across

1 DILS (4)
4 APSW (4)
7 AAMOS (5)
8 LNOY (4)
10 AILR (4)
12 EOW (3)
13 ABEHT (5)
15 AERVW (5)
17 ABC (3)

19 ADEI (4)
20 CDEO (4)
21 AILRT (5)
22 NOOS (4)
23 AKNT (4)

Down

1 LOSW (4)
2 EILS (4)
3 ADY (3)
4 ALORS (5)

5 AITW
6 EPRU (4)
9 ADMNO (5)
11 AADEH (5)
14 AENRY (5)
15 INSW (4)
16 EOTV (4)
17 ACLO (4)
18 ABEK (4)
20 ACT (3)

111

Around the Clock

Travel around the clock, one hour at a time, making twelve words all ending with the central letter. The letters to be placed in the empty squares are to be found in the segment clockwise of the number to be filled. We've completed one already, in order to get you off to a timely start…

Now take the central letter of every even-numbered word and rearrange these to form another, meaning: Computer screen pointer.

___ ___ ___ ___ ___ ___

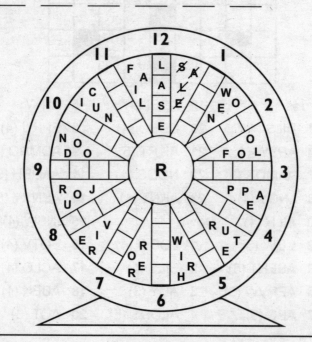

112

Around the Block

You won't need a starting block to get you under way, because it isn't a race! Just arrange the six-letter solutions to the clues into the six blocks around each clue number.

Write the answers in a clockwise or anticlockwise direction and you'll find that the last answer fits into the first; the main problem will be to decide in which square to put the first letter of each word…

1 Twice the amount
2 Suitable to eat
3 Deferred payment

4 Depression formed by an impact or explosion
5 Ruffles, folds
6 Willing to be led, obedient

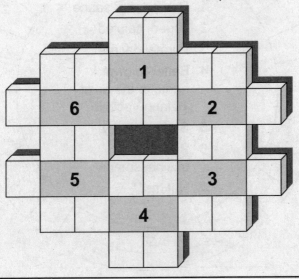

113

Roundword

Write the answer to each clue into the grid, working in a clockwise direction.

Every solution overlaps the next by either one, two, or three letters and each solution starts in its numbered section.

The solution to the final clue ends with the letter in the first square.

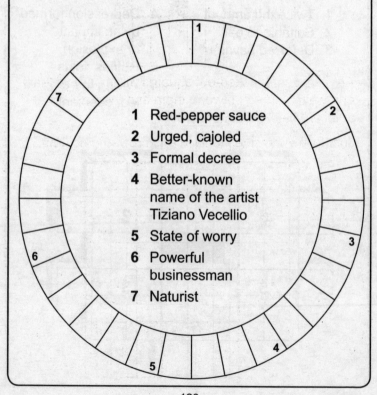

1 Red-pepper sauce
2 Urged, cajoled
3 Formal decree
4 Better-known name of the artist Tiziano Vecellio
5 State of worry
6 Powerful businessman
7 Naturist

114

Square Filler

The clues list the groups of adjacent blacked-out squares for each row and column, as you can see in this example:

2 3	■	■		■	■	■
1 2		■		■		
1 1 1	■		■		■	■
1 4	■		■	■	■	■
5	■	■	■	■	■	
1 1			■			■
	1 3	2 1	3	5	2 2	1 2 1

Any adjacent blacked-out squares must have at least one white square between them and the next set of adjacent blacked-out squares.

Just follow the clues to fill in each row and column.

2 2						
1 1 1						
6						
1 4						
3 1						
2 3						
	6	1 1 2	3	3 1	1 4	4 1

115

Dice Section

Printed onto every one of the six numbered dice are six letters (one per side), which can be rearranged to form the answer to each clue; however, some sides are invisible to you. Use the clues and write every answer into the grid. When correctly filled, the letters in the shaded squares, reading in the order 1 to 6, will spell out the title of a book by Stephen King.

1   An indigenous North American people

2   Fervent partisan

3   Official language of Israel

4   Something which is aimed at

5   Sleeping lightly

6   Poor district of a city

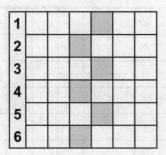

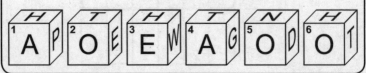

116

Pyramid Plus

Every brick in this pyramid contains a number which is the sum of the two numbers below it, so that F = A + B, etc.

Just work out the missing numbers!

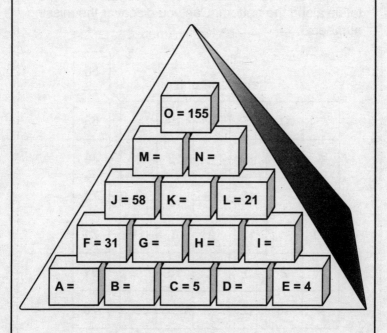

O = 155

M =   N =

J = 58   K =   L = 21

F = 31   G =   H =   I =

A =   B =   C = 5   D =   E = 4

117

Total Concentration

The blank squares below should be filled with whole numbers between 1 and 20 inclusive, any of which may occur more than once, or not at all.

The numbers in every horizontal row add up to the totals on the right, as do the two long diagonal lines; whilst those in every vertical column add up to the totals along the bottom. Can you discover the missing numbers?

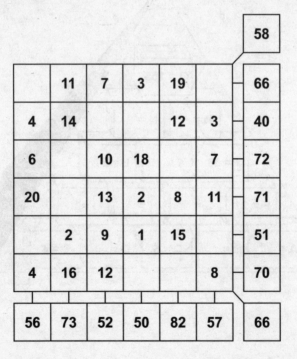

	58

	11	7	3	19		66
4	14			12	3	40
6		10	18		7	72
20		13	2	8	11	71
	2	9	1	15		51
4	16	12			8	70
56	73	52	50	82	57	66

Hexagony

Can you place the hexagons into the grid, so that where any hexagon touches another along a straight line, the contents of both triangles are the same? No rotation of any hexagon is allowed!

119

Number Fit

2 digits	3 digits	4 digits
16	204	1074
23	284	6357
25	306	
34	376	**5 digits**
53	489	12537
63	790	16509
64	803	78630
80	937	92350
98	976	

7 digits
9930467

120

Sudoku

	6			8			4	
	8	7			4	3	9	
3	4		1				5	8
4		1	2	6				
7								9
				3	7	4		5
2	7				9		8	1
	5	6	8			2	3	
	1			5			6	

121

Box Clever

When the box below is folded to form a cube, just one of the five options (A, B, C, D, or E) can be produced. Which?

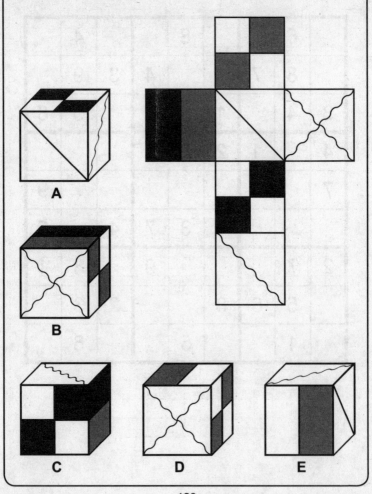

A

B

C

D

E

Sequence Conundrum

  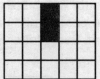

Which one of the lettered alternatives continues the sequence above?

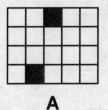

A

B

C

 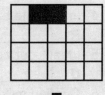

D

E

Downwords

The solutions to the clues are all six-letter words, the letters for which are contained in the grid, at the rate of one per line and in the correct order from top to bottom. Every letter is used once only.

A	F	M	R	U	Y
E	I	O	P	T	U
A	C	G	I	O	T
A	E	P	S	U	U
A	C	I	N	R	R
A	L	O	T	T	Y

1 Bee-house
   A _____

2 Debacle
   F _____

3 Shared, reciprocal
   M _____

4 Immediate past
   R _____

5 Ideally perfect country
   U _____

6 Curdled milk food
   Y _____

Sum Circle

Fill the three empty circles with the symbols +, −, and x in some order to make a sum which totals the number in the centre.

Each symbol must be used once and calculations are made in the direction of travel (clockwise).

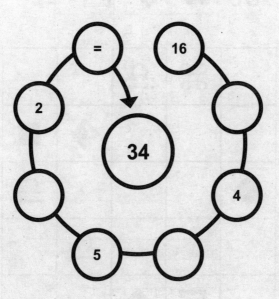

Shape Up

Each row and column of this grid should be filled with one of five different symbols, so that all five appear in that row or column.

Some are already in place – can you complete the grid?

126

Eliminator

Every oval shape in this diagram contains a different letter of the alphabet from A to K inclusive. Use the clues to determine their locations. Reference in the clues to "due" means in any location along the same horizontal or vertical line.

1 A is next to and south of F, which is next to and east of K.

2 B is next to and south of J, which is next to and east of I.

3 C is next to and east of H, which is next to and south of G.

4 D is due east of J, which is further south than H.

5 E is next to and north of K.

6 G is due west of F.

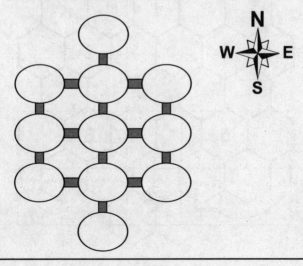

127

Hexafit

Can you place these six words into the hexagons? To fit them all in, some will have to be entered clockwise and others anticlockwise around the numbers.

Two letters have been placed already, which should give you a good start!

ABSURD   AGREED   DEEPER

ENERGY   KITTEN   TABLET

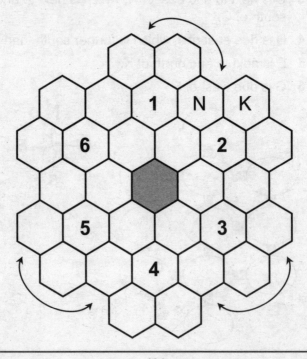

Stamp It Out!

Can you pair each of the
stamps with its correct print?

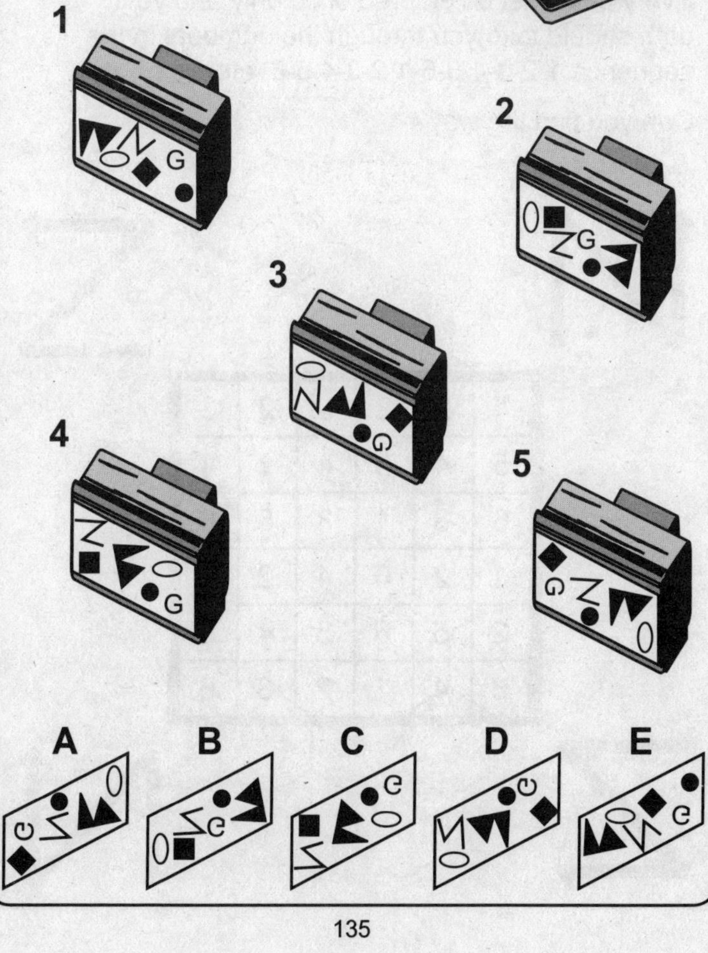

1

2

3

4

5

A **B** **C** **D** **E**

Pathfinder

The object of this puzzle is to trace a single path from the top left corner to the bottom right corner of the grid, travelling through all of the cells in either a horizontal, vertical, or diagonal direction.

Every cell must be entered once only and your path should take you through the numbers in the sequence 1-2-3-4-5-6-1-2-3-4-5-6, etc.

Can you find the way?

1	2	3	6	2	3
5	4	5	4	1	4
6	3	1	3	5	6
1	2	6	4	2	1
2	5	6	5	4	5
3	4	1	2	3	6

130

Memory Game

Study the picture below for 30 seconds and then turn to page 87.

This part of the test relates to the puzzle on page 337. Which of the following have you just seen?

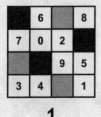

1

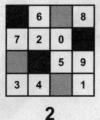

2

3

131

Shadows

Which of the shadows below is that of the kite shown here?

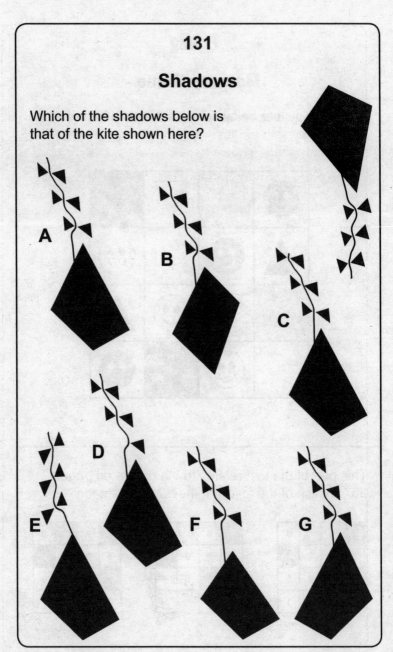

132

Jigsaw Puzzle

Which four shapes (two black and two white) can be fitted together to form the shape shown here?

The pieces may be rotated, but not flipped over.

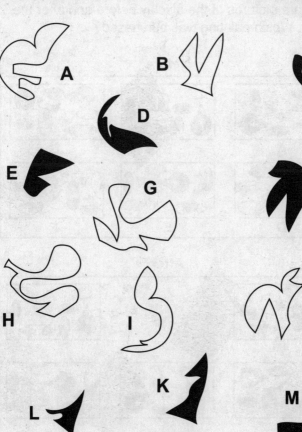

133

Buy-Buy

The Abstract Art Gallery has just sold a painting, after some deliberation by the customer, who took down each painting, turning it this way and that, before making a choice, and replacing five of the paintings haphazardly on the wall of the gallery.

Here are pictures of the display before and after the event. Which painting was purchased?

Before

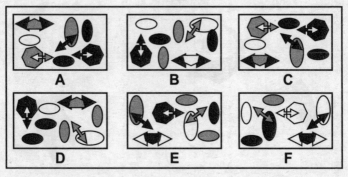

After

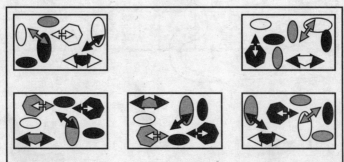

134

Sudoku

6	4		9				7	1
		5	6					4
	7		5	8	4		3	
		1	3					5
3	8						2	9
4					6	8		
	6		4	2	3		9	
8					9	3		
2	9				1		5	7

135

Word Ladder

Change one letter at a time (but not the position of any letter) to make a new word – and move from the word at the top of the ladder to the word at the bottom, using the exact number of rungs provided.

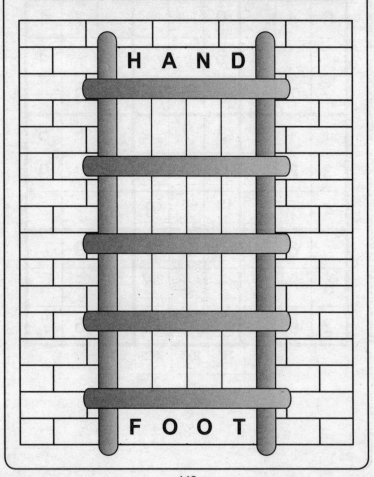

H A N D

F O O T

136

Treasure Hunt

The chart below gives directions to a hidden treasure behind the central black square in the grid.

Move the indicated number of spaces north, south, east, and west (e.g., 4N would mean four squares north) stopping at each square once only to arrive there.

At which square should you start?

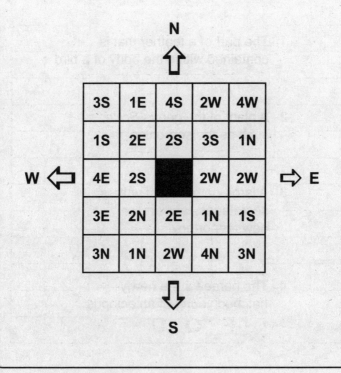

N

3S	1E	4S	2W	4W
1S	2E	2S	3S	1N
4E	2S	■	2W	2W
3E	2N	2E	1N	1S
3N	1N	2W	4N	3N

W   E

S

Wordpower

Which one of the four alternatives is the correct definition of the word shown below?

SQUILL

1 The part of a feather that is contained within the body of a bird

2 A plant of the genus *Scilla*, such as the sea-onion

3 A large gathering of writers, secretaries, lawyers, or news reporters

4 The name for the newly-hatched young of an octopus

138

Maze

Can you trace your way through this maze, without taking your pencil from the paper?

139

Wordwheel

How many words of three or more letters can you make from those in the wheel, without using plurals, abbreviations, or proper nouns in just three minutes?

The central letter must appear once in every word and no letter in a section of the wheel may be used more than once.

There is at least one nine-letter word in the wheel.

Nine-letter word(s):

Tile Twister

Place the eight tiles into the puzzle grid so that all adjacent numbers on each tile match up. Any tile may be rotated, but none may be flipped over.

4	3
2	4

1	2
4	3

1	2
1	4

4	2
3	3

1	4
2	1

3	2
4	1

3	1
3	4

1	2
1	2

				4	3
				3	1

141

Bermuda Triangle

Travel through the "Bermuda Triangle" by visiting one room at a time to collect a letter from each. You can enter the outside passageway as often as you like, but can only visit each room once.

When you've completed your tour, the 15 letters (in order) will spell out a word.

142

Shape Spotter

Which is the only shape to appear twice in the box below? You'll need a keen eye for this one, as some shapes overlap others!

143

Link Words

Fit different words into the central columns of the grid, so that each one links up with the words to either side, for example: table – lamp – shade.

When finished, read down the letters in the shaded squares to reveal another word, solving the clue below the grid.

ELASTIC					AGE
BIT					TIME
ICE					COMFORT
AIR					SMITH
BOXING					LEADER
KARATE					STICKS
FAST					ALLERGY
EARTH					HOLE

Clue: Dance hall

Word: _____

Half and Half

Pair off these groups of three letters to make eight nautical terms, each comprising six letters.

HOM   LER   AST   SAM

ANC   ISE   LOR   INA

TIL   JET   FAT   HOR

MAR   ERN   CRU   SAI

_____   _____

_____   _____

_____   _____

_____   _____

145

Couplets

The picture is of a central circle surrounded by shapes, linked to form six sets of three shapes apiece. Can you complete the puzzle by placing each of the two-letter groups below, one per shape, so that every set of three (the central circle, plus the two matching shapes diagonally opposite one another) forms a six-letter word? Whichever pair of letters you place in the central circle will appear in the middle of every word.

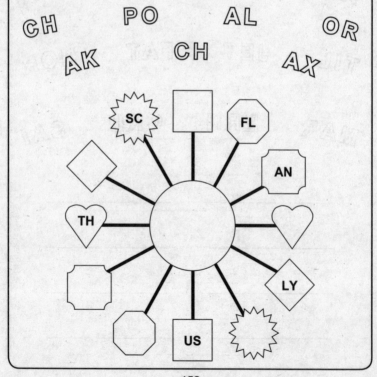

146

Keyword

On the face of it, this puzzle seems straightforward. Simply fill in the letters missing from words 1-8 and enter them into the numbered boxes, to reveal a hidden keyword.

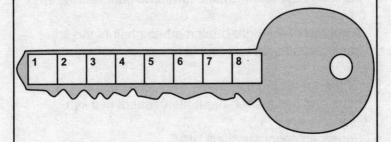

1	2	3	4	5	6	7	8	

1   R   E   __   E   C   T

2   S   I   N   F   __   L

3   A   __   S   U   R   D

4   E   N   D   __   N   G

5   T   R   A   V   __   E

6   __   V   E   N   G   E

7   __   O   T   I   C   E

8   O   B   __   A   I   N

147

Fractional Process

One summer's morning, several fishermen lined the banks of a Tennessee river.

Three-quarters of the men fished from the right-hand bank and the rest from the left-hand bank.

A quarter of the right-bank men and half of the left-bank men caught just one fish.

Of the remaining fishermen, two-thirds of the right-bank and half the left-bank men caught two fish.

Four men caught nothing at all.

There were sixteen fishermen in total. What was the total number of fish caught?

148

Cut Out

Can you pair up shapes with the squares from which they were cut? Some may have been flipped over.

1

2

3

4

5

6

A

B

C

D

E

F

149

In at the Count

Precisely how many pears are in this picture?

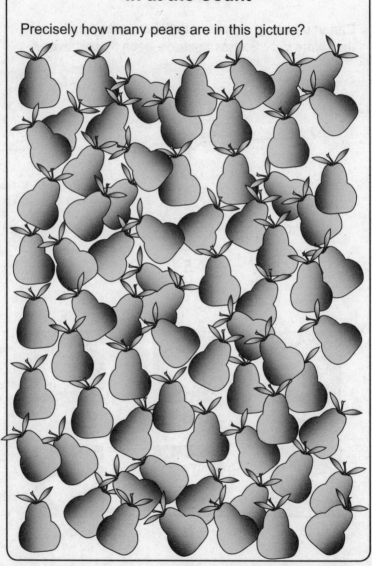

150

Follow the Thread

These fishing lines have become tangled. Can you sort out which fish has been caught by each angler?

151

James Bond Wordsearch

```
T P Q V I J A Y G O A
T A X S G T O B N O P
A S I H T A M M S A Z
R O B H B E R B L Z T
K I O D L K G D R N O
Q R J S I K G D I V T
U A D D K R J W A P D
S D D Z R G R R Q G N
M F O U M M G J A W S
B B E L K A S O R S G
L I Q E S X F C Q J O
```

DARIO   MR KIL

DR NO   MR WINT

GADGETS   ODDJOB

JAWS   ROSA KLEBB

KRATT   VARGAS

MATHIS   VIJAY

MR KIDD   ZAO

152

Sequence Conundrum

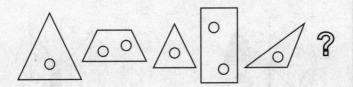

Which one of the lettered alternatives continues the sequence above?

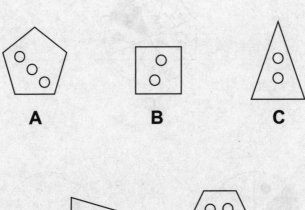

A   **B**   **C**

D   **E**

Odd One Out

Which is the odd one out – and why?

A

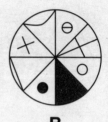

B

C

D

E

154

Sudoku

		8		1		4	2	5
		4	5	7	9			
		6	2		8			
	6		7		2			4
7		2				3		1
4			6		1		9	
			9		3	1		
			4	8	5	9		
5	3	9		6		8		

155

Wordfit

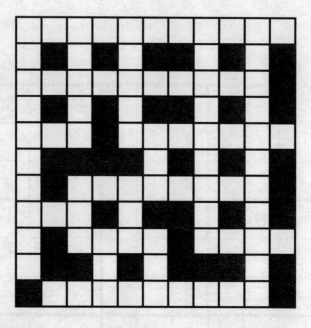

3 letters
ALL
EGG
ICE
ILL
OAK
RAY
VET

4 letters
DROP
TAKE

5 letters
MUMMY
SHELF

7 letters
FIGURED

8 letters
VIOLATES

9 letters
EXHAUSTED
RELIGIOUS

10 letters
ADMIRATION
MEMBERSHIP

11 letters
ATMOSPHERIC
IMPRESSIONS

156

Spot the Difference

Which of these is different from the rest – and how?

1

2

3

4

5

6

Character Assignation

Fill in the Across clues in this crossword in the normal way. Then read down the diagonal line of eight squares, to reveal:
A cartoon character created by Hanna and Barbera (two words).

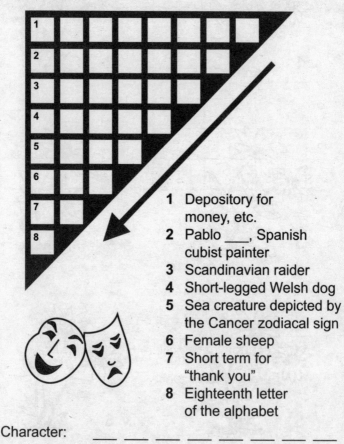

1 Depository for money, etc.
2 Pablo ___, Spanish cubist painter
3 Scandinavian raider
4 Short-legged Welsh dog
5 Sea creature depicted by the Cancer zodiacal sign
6 Female sheep
7 Short term for "thank you"
8 Eighteenth letter of the alphabet

Character: ___ ___ ___ ___ ___ ___ ___ ___

158

Pyracross

Solve the clues on each level of the pyramid and reveal the word in the central column of bricks, a clue for which is: City in Washington, USA.

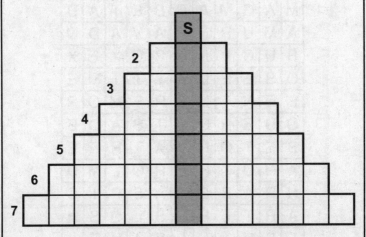

2 Wager

3 Davy Crockett's last battle

4 Country, capital Vienna

5 First man to set foot on the moon

6 Pseudonym of William F. Cody (7,4)

7 European principality

HIDDEN WORD: _____

Do It Yourself!

The listed words all appear in this crossword – you just need to blank out the unwanted squares…

M	A	G	M	A	R	B	E	T	A	B
A	M	U	R	B	R	A	V	A	D	O
B	U	G	L	E	R	B	O	X	E	X
O	S	E	E	D	A	Y	T	I	M	E
B	E	N	T	U	B	R	E	M	O	R
O	D	E	R	O	O	T	S	A	D	E
B	E	T	O	R	V	A	T	R	E	E
A	N	O	T	H	E	R	O	L	M	D
N	R	A	B	E	T	A	S	P	I	C
A	R	T	L	E	S	S	L	O	S	H
L	C	H	I	L	L	P	A	N	E	L

ABED	BENT	OATH
ABOVE	BOXER	PANEL
AMUSED	BRAVADO	RASP
ANOTHER	BUGLE	ROOTS
ARTLESS	DAYTIME	TAXI
ASPIC	DEMISE	TEST
BABY	HEEL	TREE
BANAL	MAGMA	TROT

160

Letters Crossword

Each clue consists of letters in alphabetical order.
Rearrange these to form words, then fill the grid.

Across
- **1** ALNW (4)
- **3** FIST (4)
- **5** AKS (3)
- **7** EIOOPPRSS (9)
- **11** AER (3)
- **12** BEEELPR (7)
- **15** CTU (3)
- **17** AAEJKLRWY (9)
- **20** EEY (3)
- **21** AFRT (4)
- **22** DTUY (4)

Down
- **1** ELOP (4)
- **2** ANP (3)
- **3** IKS (3)
- **4** KSTU (4)
- **6** ADEMOSY (7)
- **8** BOR (3)
- **9** ALLRY (5)
- **10** CEKPS (5)
- **13** ERU (3)
- **14** AAJR (4)
- **16** ARTY (4)
- **18** ETW (3)
- **19** DEL (3)

161

Around the Clock

Travel around the clock, one hour at a time, making twelve words all ending with the central letter. The letters to be placed in the empty squares are to be found in the segment clockwise of the number to be filled. We've completed one already, in order to get you off to a timely start…

Now take the central letter of every even-numbered word and rearrange these to form another, meaning: Filament.

____   ____   ____   ____   ____   ____

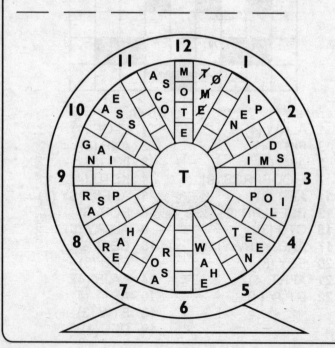

162

Around the Block

You won't need a starting block to get you under way, because it isn't a race! Just arrange the six-letter solutions to the clues into the six blocks around each clue number.

Write the answers in a clockwise or anticlockwise direction and you'll find that the last answer fits into the first; the main problem will be to decide in which square to put the first letter of each word…

1 Popular game bird
2 Spanish afternoon nap
3 Sloping letter
4 Make up one's mind
5 Ocean floor
6 Awaken, excite

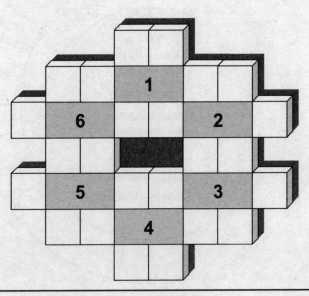

163

Roundword

Write the answer to each clue into the grid, working in a clockwise direction.

Every solution overlaps the next by either one, two, or three letters and each solution starts in its numbered section.

The solution to the final clue ends with the letter in the first square.

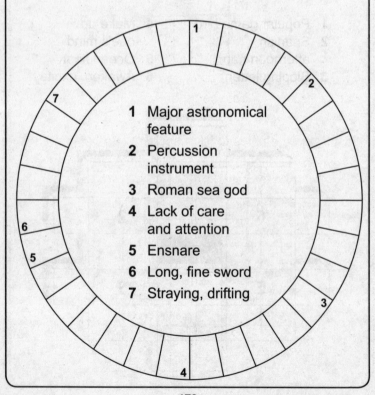

1 Major astronomical feature

2 Percussion instrument

3 Roman sea god

4 Lack of care and attention

5 Ensnare

6 Long, fine sword

7 Straying, drifting

164

Square Filler

The clues list the groups of adjacent blacked-out squares for each row and column, as you can see in this example:

Any adjacent blacked-out squares must have at least one white square between them and the next set of adjacent blacked-out squares.

Just follow the clues to fill in each row and column.

165

Dice Section

Printed onto every one of the six numbered dice are six letters (one per side), which can be rearranged to form the answer to each clue; however, some sides are invisible to you. Use the clues and write every answer into the grid. When correctly filled, the letters in the shaded squares, reading in the order 1 to 6, will spell out a weapon.

1 Aide, assistant

2 Author

3 Liqueur made from cherries

4 Powerful, virile

5 Soak up

6 Unit of liquid measurement

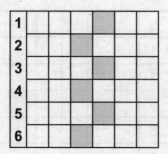

166

Pyramid Plus

Every brick in this pyramid contains a number which is the sum of the two numbers below it, so that F = A + B, etc.

Just work out the missing numbers!

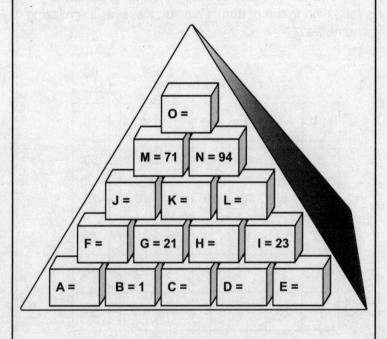

O =

M = 71   N = 94

J =   K =   L =

F =   G = 21   H =   I = 23

A =   B = 1   C =   D =   E =

167

Total Concentration

The blank squares below should be filled with whole numbers between 1 and 20 inclusive, any of which may occur more than once, or not at all.

The numbers in every horizontal row add up to the totals on the right, as do the two long diagonal lines; whilst those in every vertical column add up to the totals along the bottom. Can you discover the missing numbers?

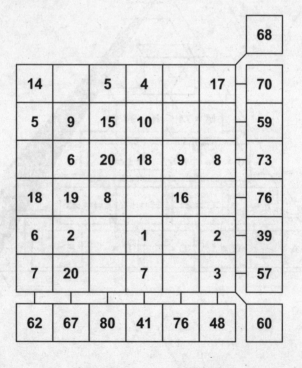

						68
14		5	4		17	**70**
5	9	15	10			**59**
	6	20	18	9	8	**73**
18	19	8		16		**76**
6	2		1		2	**39**
7	20		7		3	**57**
62	**67**	**80**	**41**	**76**	**48**	**60**

168

Hexagony

Can you place the hexagons into the grid, so that where any hexagon touches another along a straight line, the contents of both triangles are the same? No rotation of any hexagon is allowed!

169

Number Fit

2 digits	3 digits	5 digits
18	127	16788
28	243	29477
33	334	40823
51	401	45022
60	446	52200
88		
97	**4 digits**	**6 digits**
	1264	807763
	1307	893622
	2097	
	3730	**7 digits**
	8364	3350067

170

Sudoku

	5			8		2		
1		3	4		6			7
		7	3		9			5
	1	8	5					4
9				4				1
2					7	3	6	
5			1		2	6		
8			6		4	5		9
		1		9			7	

Box Clever

When the box below is folded to form a cube, just one of the five options (A, B, C, D, or E) can be produced. Which?

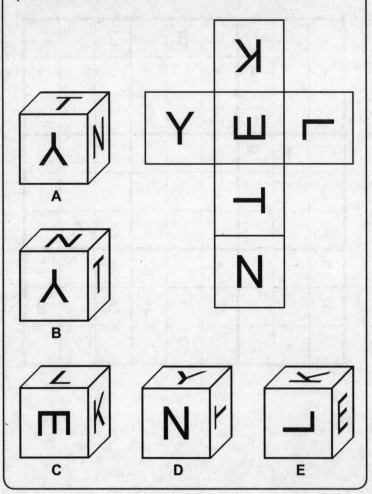

172

Sequence Conundrum

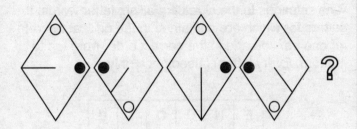

Which one of the lettered alternatives continues the sequence above?

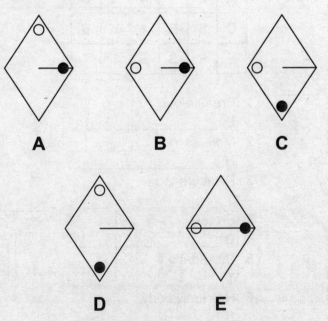

173

Downwords

The solutions to the clues are all six-letter words, the letters for which are contained in the grid, at the rate of one per line and in the correct order from top to bottom. Every letter is used once only.

E	H	J	O	T	U
B	H	O	R	U	X
A	E	H	J	L	N
A	E	I	K	N	S
C	E	E	I	L	U
E	R	S	S	T	T

1 Breathe out
   E _____

2 More sacred
   H _____

3 Pleasure trip
   J _____

4 Protest
   O _____

5 Dissertation
   T _____

6 Heavenly body
   U _____

174

Sum Circle

Fill the three empty circles with the symbols +, −, and x in some order to make a sum which totals the number in the centre.

Each symbol must be used once and calculations are made in the direction of travel (clockwise).

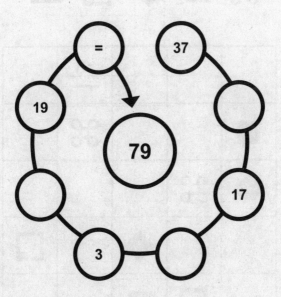

Shape Up

Each row and column of this grid should be filled with one of five different symbols, so that all five appear in that row or column.

Some are already in place – can you complete the grid?

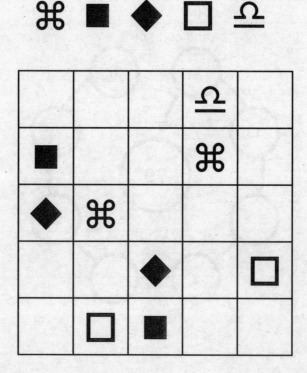

176

Eliminator

Every oval shape in this diagram contains a different letter of the alphabet from A to K inclusive. Use the clues to determine their locations. Reference in the clues to "due" means in any location along the same horizontal or vertical line.

1 A is next to and south of D, which is next to and west of B.

2 C is next to and south of K, which is next to and west of H.

3 E is next to and north of G, which is next to and east of I.

4 F is next to and north of J, which is due east of D.

5 H is further south than B.

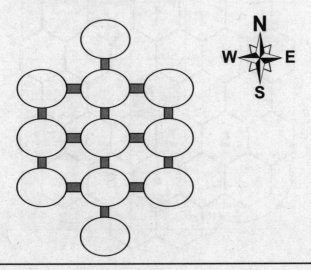

177

Hexafit

Can you place these six words into the hexagons? To fit them all in, some will have to be entered clockwise and others anticlockwise around the numbers.

Two letters have been placed already, which should give you a good start!

DIETED   DIESEL   GLOWED

POWDER   PRAISE   TANGLE

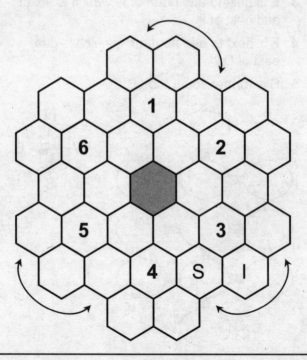

178

Stamp It Out!

Can you pair each of the stamps with its correct print?

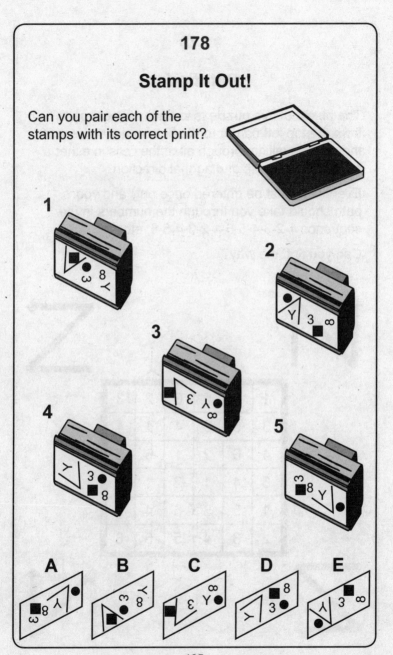

Pathfinder

The object of this puzzle is to trace a single path from the top left corner to the bottom right corner of the grid, travelling through all of the cells in either a horizontal, vertical, or diagonal direction.

Every cell must be entered once only and your path should take you through the numbers in the sequence 1-2-3-4-5-6-1-2-3-4-5-6, etc.

Can you find the way?

1	2	5	6	2	3
3	5	3	4	1	4
4	6	2	1	6	5
6	4	1	2	1	2
1	5	3	6	4	3
2	3	4	5	5	6

180

Memory Game

Study the picture below for 30 seconds and then turn to page 337.

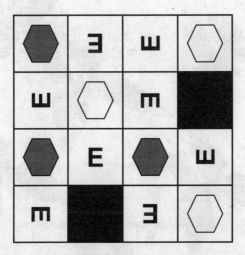

This part of the test relates to the puzzle on page 387. Which of the following have you just seen?

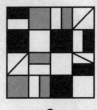

| 1 | 2 | 3 |

181

Shadows

Which of the shadows below is that of the butterfly shown here?

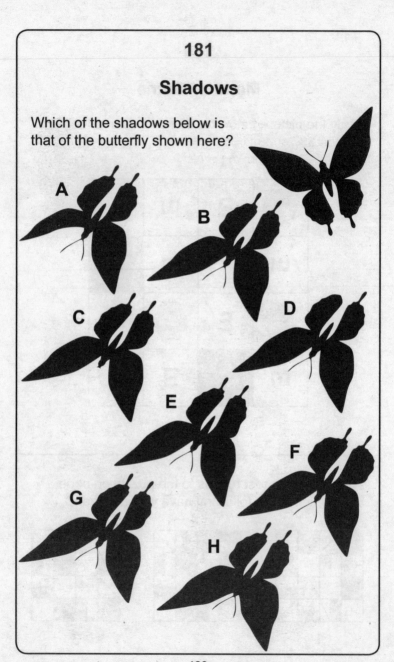

A

B

C

D

E

F

G

H

182

Jigsaw Puzzle

Which four shapes (two black and two white) can be fitted together to form the shape shown here?

The pieces may be rotated, but not flipped over.

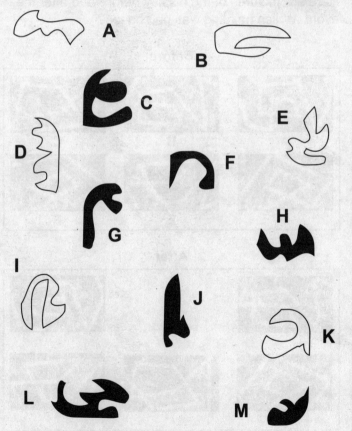

A

B

C

D

E

F

G

H

I

J

K

L

M

Buy-Buy

The Abstract Art Gallery has just sold a painting, after some deliberation by the customer, who took down each painting, turning it this way and that, before making a choice, and replacing five of the paintings haphazardly on the wall of the gallery.

Here are pictures of the display before and after the event. Which painting was purchased?

Before

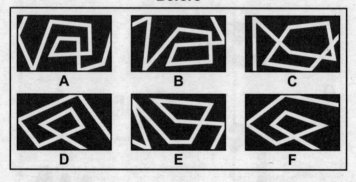

After

Sudoku

	6		1		5			
	5			4		9	3	1
	3		9	2	8			
		3	6		4			8
	1	2				4	7	
6			2		1	3		
			3	5	9		8	
7	8	9		6			5	
			8		7		4	

185

Word Ladder

Change one letter at a time (but not the position of any letter) to make a new word – and move from the word at the top of the ladder to the word at the bottom, using the exact number of rungs provided.

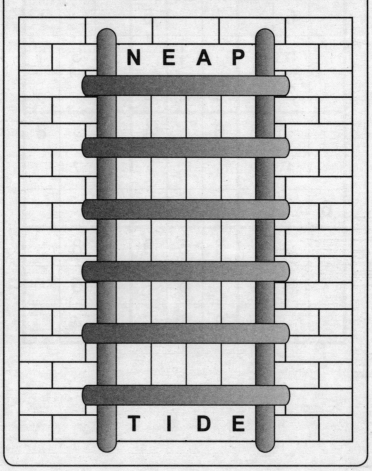

N E A P

T I D E

186

Treasure Hunt

The chart below gives directions to a hidden treasure behind the central black square in the grid.

Move the indicated number of spaces north, south, east, and west (e.g., 4N would mean four squares north) stopping at each square once only to arrive there.

At which square should you start?

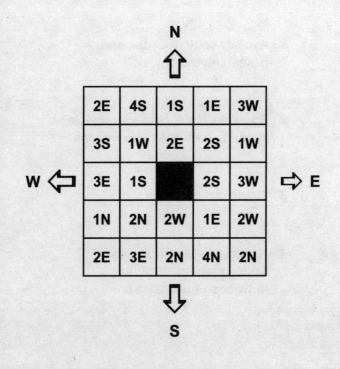

Wordpower

Which one of the four alternatives is the correct definition of the word shown below?

ANCHORITE

1 A minor deity of Greek and Roman mythology

2 An explosive substance especially suited to undersea excavations

3 A religious recluse

4 A barnacle-like crustacean which attaches itself only to wooden-hulled boats

188

Maze

Can you trace your way through this maze, without taking your pencil from the paper?

Wordwheel

How many words of three or more letters can you make from those in the wheel, without using plurals, abbreviations, or proper nouns in just three minutes?

The central letter must appear once in every word and no letter in a section of the wheel may be used more than once.

There is at least one nine-letter word in the wheel.

Nine-letter word(s):

Tile Twister

Place the eight tiles into the puzzle grid so that all adjacent numbers on each tile match up. Any tile may be rotated, but none may be flipped over.

4	2
1	3

2	4
1	3

2	1
4	3

4	3
3	1

3	2
3	1

4	4
2	2

3	4
4	2

3	2
2	1

3	3				
2	2				

Bermuda Triangle

Travel through the "Bermuda Triangle" by visiting one room at a time to collect a letter from each. You can enter the outside passageway as often as you like, but can only visit each room once.

When you've completed your tour, the 15 letters (in order) will spell out a word.

192

Shape Spotter

Which is the only shape to appear twice in the box below? You'll need a keen eye for this one, as some shapes overlap others!

Link Words

Fit different words into the central columns of the grid, so that each one links up with the words to either side, for example: table – lamp – shade.

When finished, read down the letters in the shaded squares to reveal another word, solving the clue below the grid.

CORAL					KNOT
THREAD					FACED
HARD					SHAPE
FULL					PRESS
BRAIN					BASIN
ANGEL					HOOK
BATHING					CASE
FREE					BACK

Clue: Steadfast in allegiance

Word: _____

Half and Half

Pair off these groups of three letters to make eight drinks, each comprising six letters.

SKY   COG   FEE   SCH

CLA   SHE   BRA   NAC

PPA   NDY   WHI   GRA

KIR   COF   RET   RRY

_____   _____

_____   _____

_____   _____

_____   _____

195

Couplets

The picture is of a central circle surrounded by shapes, linked to form six sets of three shapes apiece. Can you complete the puzzle by placing each of the two-letter groups below, one per shape, so that every set of three (the central circle, plus the two matching shapes diagonally opposite one another) forms a six-letter word? Whichever pair of letters you place in the central circle will appear in the middle of every word.

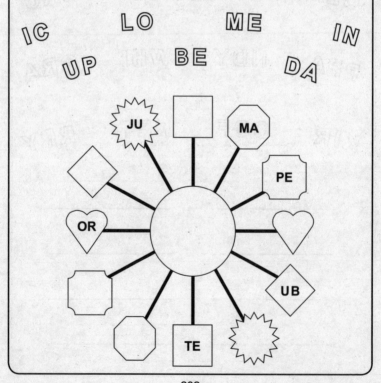

IC   LO   ME   IN
UP   BE   DA

JU   MA   PE   OR   UB   TE

196

Keyword

On the face of it, this puzzle seems straightforward. Simply fill in the letters missing from words 1-8 and enter them into the numbered boxes, to reveal a hidden keyword.

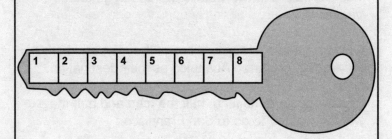

1	2	3	4	5	6	7	8

1 **A** **L** __ **L** **U** __ **E**

2 **P** **R** __ **F** **I** **X**

3 __ **E** **S** **S** **O** **N**

4 __ **R** **G** **E** **N** **T**

5 **O** **D** **I** **O** **U** __

6 **K** __ **L** __ **L** **E** **R**

7 **A** **B** __ **U** **N** **D**

8 **W** **A** __ **D** **E** **R**

Fractional Process

Twenty people (ten men and ten women) from the town's Rotary Club decided to take a weekend trip, but they couldn't agree where to go.

Half the men and two women wanted to go to Las Vegas.

Of the remaining people, three of the men and half the women preferred Acapulco as their destination.

Of the people remaining, half the men and half the women wanted to go to San Francisco.

The remaining people were completely undecided and wanted more time to think about it.

How many people were undecided?

198

Cut Out

Can you pair up shapes with the squares from which they were cut? Some may have been flipped over.

1

2

3

4

5

6

A

B

C

D

E

F

In at the Count

Precisely how many yachts are in this picture?

200

Follow the Thread

These fishing lines have become tangled. Can you sort out which fish has been caught by each angler?

201

Computing Wordsearch

```
X R K U I R W Y J L S
N F R A G M E N T A E
L O L N M B H W O U T
H B I D D A N Z O T Y
S J Q T K S I D D R B
Q E D L A I R E S I D
B C G R L C C X N V I
A T A L U E O M T C H
O T E C H N O L O G Y
U H N M G N J N L S K
S L A V E O T D S A E
```

ALLOCATION	OBJECT
BASIC	SERIAL
BYTES	SHELL
CMOS	SLAVE
DISK	TECHNOLOGY
FRAGMENT	VIRTUAL
ICON	WORD

202

Sequence Conundrum

Which one of the lettered alternatives continues the sequence above?

A

B

C

D

Odd One Out

Which is the odd one out – and why?

A

B

C

D

E

F

204

Sudoku

1				4	2	7		
	2		7			8	9	
4		8			5		3	
			5	3		6	8	9
		7				1		
5	6	9		8	4			
	8		3			4		7
	5	2			1		6	
		6	2	9				3

205

Wordfit

3 letters
GNU
NIB
RID

4 letters
DOOR
EDDY
GORE
OBEY
STEP

5 letters
ABHOR
EMPTY

6 letters
DARKEN
ONWARD

7 letters
CUNNING
REFEREE

9 letters
PEPPERONI

10 letters
PRECAUTION

11 letters
INTROVERTED
MASTERPIECE
PERFORMANCE

206

Spot the Difference

Which of these is different from the rest – and how?

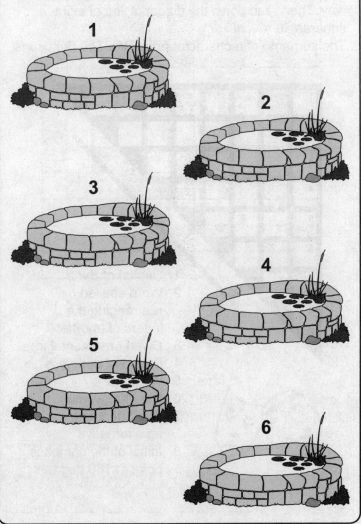

1

2

3

4

5

6

207

Character Assignation

Fill in the Across clues in this crossword in the normal way. Then read down the diagonal line of eight squares, to reveal:
The surname of a character from TV's *The Simpsons*.

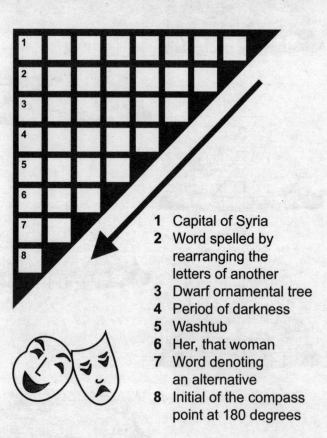

1 Capital of Syria
2 Word spelled by rearranging the letters of another
3 Dwarf ornamental tree
4 Period of darkness
5 Washtub
6 Her, that woman
7 Word denoting an alternative
8 Initial of the compass point at 180 degrees

Character: _ _ _ _ _ _ _ _

208

Pyracross

Solve the clues on each level of the pyramid and reveal the word in the central column of bricks, a clue for which is: City in Tennessee, USA.

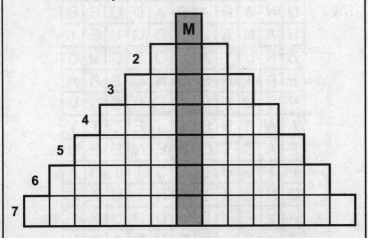

2 Sleeping place

3 Walt Disney's elephant with huge ears

4 Capital of Libya

5 German composer, Ludwig van ___

6 Myopic (4-7)

7 Capital of Missouri, USA (9,4)

HIDDEN WORD: _____

209

Do It Yourself!

The listed words all appear in this crossword – you just need to blank out the unwanted squares…

U	N	W	R	A	P	A	D	O	R	B
B	A	N	A	L	I	D	O	L	E	I
B	R	U	T	A	L	O	A	D	U	G
E	R	T	H	B	O	N	C	E	R	A
P	O	M	E	E	T	E	R	S	U	M
A	W	A	R	D	I	J	E	T	T	Y
F	A	S	T	O	P	E	N	E	E	D
L	I	L	U	L	L	S	T	I	N	A
O	N	E	X	T	A	N	I	M	A	L
A	V	E	V	E	N	D	R	U	N	E
T	I	P	I	S	T	R	E	A	T	Y

AFLOAT	EVEN	ORB
ANIMAL	IDOL	PILOT
ASLEEP	JETTY	PLANT
AWARD	LULL	RATHER
BIGAMY	NARROW	TENANT
BRUTAL	OLDEST	TIP
DUG	ONCE	TREATY
ENTIRE	ONE	UNWRAP

210

Letters Crossword

Each clue consists of letters in alphabetical order.
Rearrange these to form words, then fill the grid.

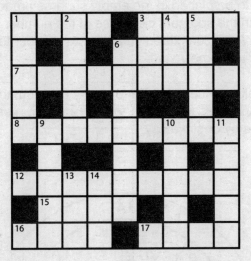

Across
- **1** ACEN (4)
- **3** AEGR (4)
- **6** AFIR (4)
- **7** ACDEMMNOR (9)
- **8** AAAILNSST (9)
- **12** CEEEIXTUV (9)
- **15** ERTU (4)
- **16** ACHR (4)
- **17** IKNT (4)

Down
- **1** ACCOO (5)
- **2** AEMNS (5)
- **3** ANR (3)
- **4** ADI (3)
- **5** EEGNR (5)
- **6** AEFGITU (7)
- **9** HISTX (5)
- **10** AIGLN (5)
- **11** EFHTT (5)
- **13** AER (3)
- **14** CRU (3)

211

Around the Clock

Travel around the clock, one hour at a time, making twelve words all ending with the central letter. The letters to be placed in the empty squares are to be found in the segment clockwise of the number to be filled. We've completed one already, in order to get you off to a timely start…

Now take the central letter of every even-numbered word and rearrange these to form another, meaning: To pass by or slip away.

___ ___ ___ ___ ___ ___

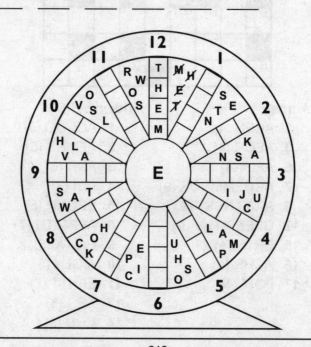

212

Around the Block

You won't need a starting block to get you under way, because it isn't a race! Just arrange the six-letter solutions to the clues into the six blocks around each clue number.

Write the answers in a clockwise or anticlockwise direction and you'll find that the last answer fits into the first; the main problem will be to decide in which square to put the first letter of each word…

1 Ghostly supernatural being
2 Equality (in pay, etc.)
3 Large, constricting snake
4 Straw roofing material
5 Place of worship
6 Grassy plains of Argentina

213

Roundword

Write the answer to each clue into the grid, working in a clockwise direction.

Every solution overlaps the next by either one, two, or three letters and each solution starts in its numbered section.

The solution to the final clue ends with the letter in the first square.

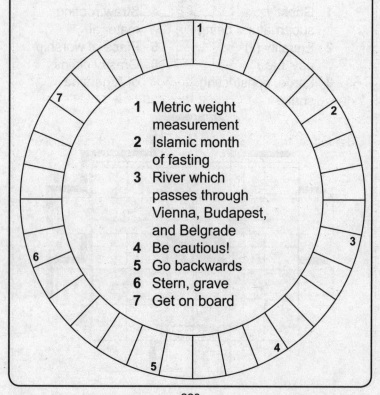

1 Metric weight measurement
2 Islamic month of fasting
3 River which passes through Vienna, Budapest, and Belgrade
4 Be cautious!
5 Go backwards
6 Stern, grave
7 Get on board

Square Filler

The clues list the groups of adjacent blacked-out squares for each row and column, as you can see in this example:

2 3						
1 2						
1 1 1						
1 4						
5						
1 1						
	1 3	2 1	3	5	2 2	1 2 1

Any adjacent blacked-out squares must have at least one white square between them and the next set of adjacent blacked-out squares.

Just follow the clues to fill in each row and column.

2 1						
6						
4						
6						
3 1						
2 1 1						
	2 3	2 3	4	3 1	4	5

Dice Section

Printed onto every one of the six numbered dice are six letters (one per side), which can be rearranged to form the answer to each clue; however, some sides are invisible to you. Use the clues and write every answer into the grid. When correctly filled, the letters in the shaded squares, reading in the order 1 to 6, will spell out a Canadian city.

1 Annul, rescind

2 Lengthen

3 Thrown away, not used to good advantage

4 Commander

5 Sleepy

6 Mythical fire-breather

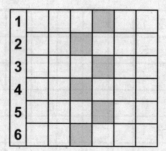

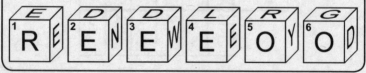

216

Pyramid Plus

Every brick in this pyramid contains a number which is the sum of the two numbers below it, so that F = A + B, etc.

Just work out the missing numbers!

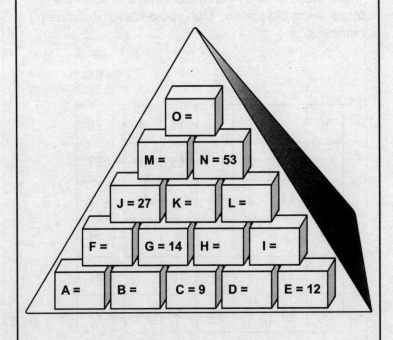

Total Concentration

The blank squares below should be filled with whole numbers between 1 and 20 inclusive, any of which may occur more than once, or not at all.

The numbers in every horizontal row add up to the totals on the right, as do the two long diagonal lines; whilst those in every vertical column add up to the totals along the bottom. Can you discover the missing numbers?

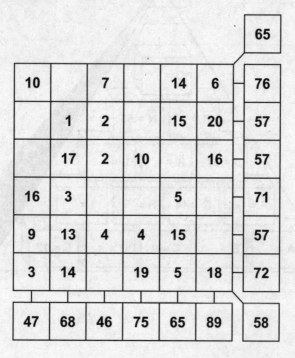

						65
10		7		14	6	76
	1	2		15	20	57
	17	2	10		16	57
16	3			5		71
9	13	4	4	15		57
3	14		19	5	18	72
47	68	46	75	65	89	58

Hexagony

Can you place the hexagons into the grid, so that where any hexagon touches another along a straight line, the contents of both triangles are the same? No rotation of any hexagon is allowed!

Number Fit

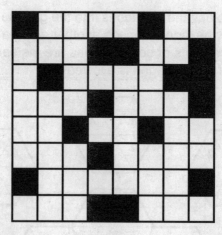

2 digits	3 digits	4 digits
24	165	2243
39	321	5834
44	665	6123
51	721	7679
59	736	
71	849	**5 digits**
72	867	24236
94	902	33947
	923	48450
		73310

6 digits
360041

220

Sudoku

5	6	8			2			
	4			5		1		2
1		3	9	8				7
				7	3		9	
	7	6				3	2	
	9		4	6				
2				3	8	6		4
7		5		4			3	
			1			8	5	9

Box Clever

When the box below is folded to form a cube, just one of the five options (A, B, C, D, or E) can be produced. Which?

A

B

C

D

E

222

Sequence Conundrum

Which one of the lettered alternatives continues the sequence above?

A

B

C

D

229

Downwords

The solutions to the clues are all six-letter words, the letters for which are contained in the grid, at the rate of one per line and in the correct order from top to bottom. Every letter is used once only.

G	I	L	N	S	V
E	I	I	L	M	R
B	O	O	P	Q	S
E	H	P	T	U	U
D	L	N	O	P	T
A	E	O	R	U	Y

1 Cave
   G _____

2 Get in the way
   I _____

3 Strong drink
   L _____

4 Interstellar cloud
   N _____

5 Slapdash
   S _____

6 Hindu deity
   V _____

Sum Circle

Fill the three empty circles with the symbols +, −, and x in some order to make a sum which totals the number in the centre.

Each symbol must be used once and calculations are made in the direction of travel (clockwise).

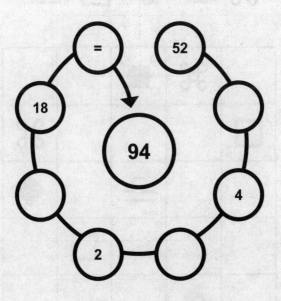

225

Shape Up

Each row and column of this grid should be filled with one of five different symbols, so that all five appear in that row or column.

Some are already in place – can you complete the grid?

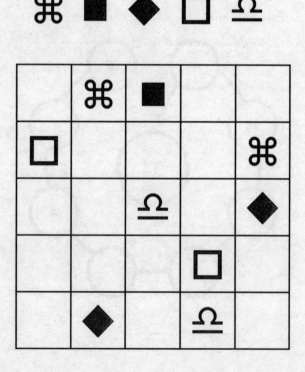

226

Eliminator

Every oval shape in this diagram contains a different letter of the alphabet from A to K inclusive. Use the clues to determine their locations. Reference in the clues to "due" means in any location along the same horizontal or vertical line.

1. A is due north of G, which is next to and east of D.

2. D is due south of C and due north of F.

3. E is due east of I, which is due north of H.

4. G is further south than B.

5. J is next to and west of C, which is due north of K.

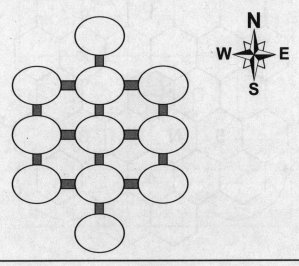

Hexafit

Can you place these six words into the hexagons? To fit them all in, some will have to be entered clockwise and others anticlockwise around the numbers.

Two letters have been placed already, which should give you a good start!

CINDER   DERIVE   ESCAPE

SENIOR   SILVER   SUPPER

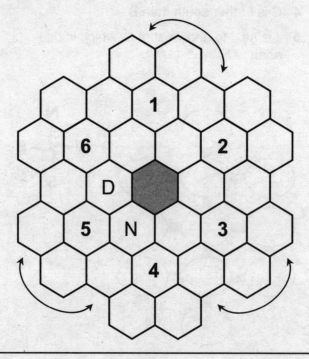

Stamp It Out!

Can you pair each of the
stamps with its correct print?

1

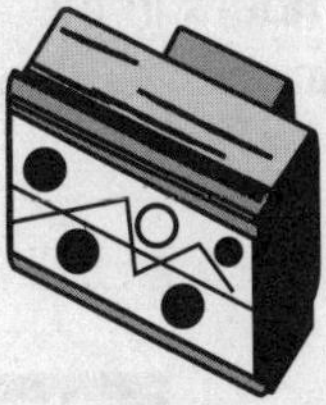

2

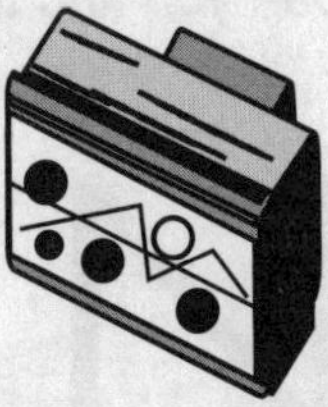

3

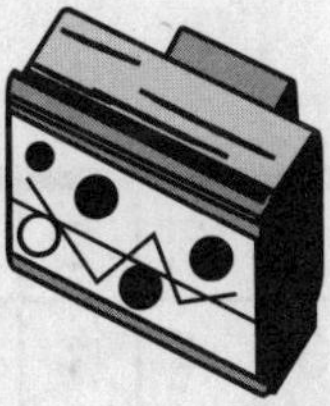

4

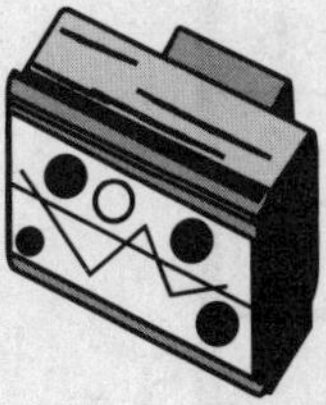

5

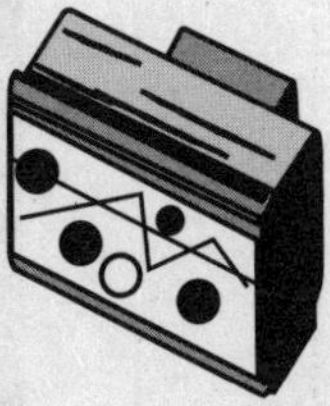

A   B   C   D   E

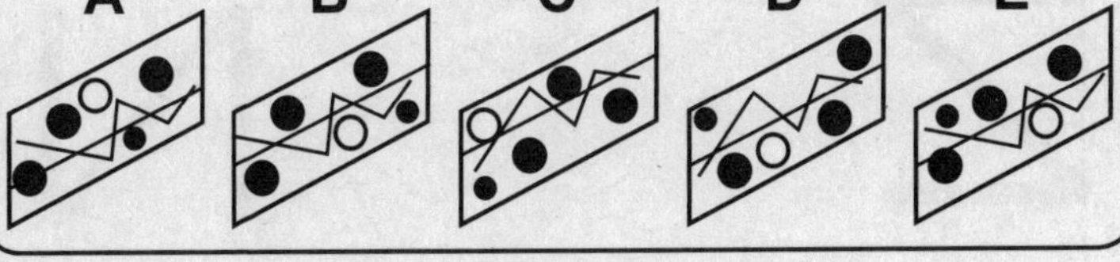

Pathfinder

The object of this puzzle is to trace a single path from the top left corner to the bottom right corner of the grid, travelling through all of the cells in either a horizontal, vertical, or diagonal direction.

Every cell must be entered once only and your path should take you through the numbers in the sequence 1-2-3-4-5-6-1-2-3-4-5-6, etc.

Can you find the way?

1	5	6	2	4	5
2	3	4	1	3	6
6	5	4	1	6	1
1	3	2	5	4	2
3	2	6	3	4	3
4	5	1	2	5	6

Memory Game

Study the picture below for 30 seconds and then turn to page 387.

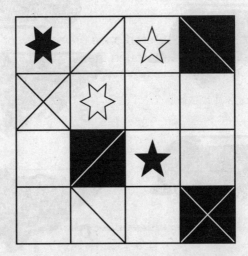

This part of the test relates to the puzzle on page 37. Which of the following have you just seen?

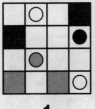

1

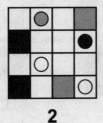

2

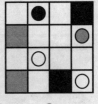

3

231

Shadows

Which of the shadows below is that of the biker shown here?

A

B

C

D

E

F

G

H

Jigsaw Puzzle

Which four shapes (two black and two white) can be fitted together to form the shape shown here?

The pieces may be rotated, but not flipped over.

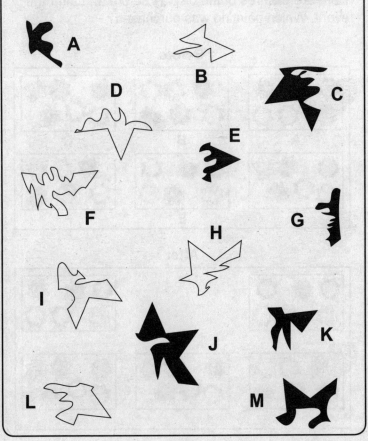

Buy-Buy

The Abstract Art Gallery has just sold a painting, after some deliberation by the customer, who took down each painting, turning it this way and that, before making a choice, and replacing five of the paintings haphazardly on the wall of the gallery.

Here are pictures of the display before and after the event. Which painting was purchased?

Before

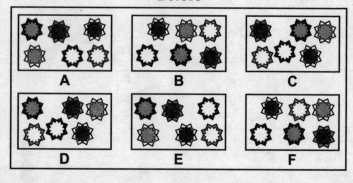

After

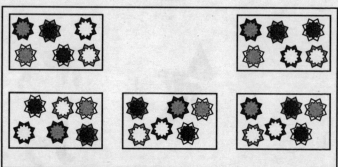

234

Sudoku

	4	2						1
			1	3	5			
7	3			2		9		8
4	5	7	2			8		
	2		3		7		1	
		9			8	6	7	2
1		5		8			3	9
			7	6	3			
8						4	2	

Word Ladder

Change one letter at a time (but not the position of any letter) to make a new word – and move from the word at the top of the ladder to the word at the bottom, using the exact number of rungs provided.

236

Treasure Hunt

The chart below gives directions to a hidden treasure behind the central black square in the grid.

Move the indicated number of spaces north, south, east, and west (e.g., 4N would mean four squares north) stopping at each square once only to arrive there.

At which square should you start?

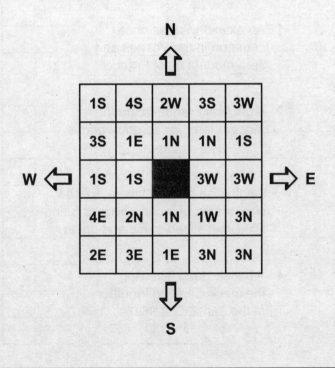

Wordpower

Which one of the four alternatives is the correct
definition of the word shown below?

ENTRECHAT

1 An extinct wild cat once
common in the Vosges and
Jura mountains of France

2 A general French-language
modern term for an entry-phone

3 A beefsteak which is scored
lengthwise several times (like the
claw marks of a cat), the cuts being
filled with sliced garlic and onion

4 A balletic leap involving
the quick clapping together
of the dancer's heels

238

Maze

Can you trace your way through this maze, without taking your pencil from the paper?

Wordwheel

How many words of three or more letters can you make from those in the wheel, without using plurals, abbreviations, or proper nouns in just three minutes?

The central letter must appear once in every word and no letter in a section of the wheel may be used more than once.

There is at least one nine-letter word in the wheel.

Nine-letter word(s):

240

Tile Twister

Place the eight tiles into the puzzle grid so that all adjacent numbers on each tile match up. Any tile may be rotated, but none may be flipped over.

3	3
2	1

4	2
1	4

2	2
3	1

2	1
3	1

3	3
4	2

1	4
2	4

4	2
1	3

3	4
2	1

		2	2		
		1	4		

241

Bermuda Triangle

Travel through the "Bermuda Triangle" by visiting one room at a time to collect a letter from each. You can enter the outside passageway as often as you like, but can only visit each room once.

When you've completed your tour, the 15 letters (in order) will spell out a word.

242

Shape Spotter

Which is the only shape to appear twice in the box below? You'll need a keen eye for this one, as some shapes overlap others!

243

Link Words

Fit different words into the central columns of the grid, so that each one links up with the words to either side, for example: table – lamp – shade.

When finished, read down the letters in the shaded squares to reveal another word, solving the clue below the grid.

ADULT					WINKED
DOUBLE					STRAP
GRAPE					YARD
PAY					STREAM
RAIL					RUNNER
DOLLAR					BOARD
CAPE					SHIP
COMMON					NIGHT

Clue: Separating

Word: _____

250

244

Half and Half

Pair off these groups of three letters to make eight countries, each comprising six letters.

BEL   DAN   TAI   ISR

FRA   WAN   ADA   BIA

ECE   IZE   AEL   NCE

ZAM   CAN   JOR   GRE

_____   _____

_____   _____

_____   _____

_____   _____

245

Couplets

The picture is of a central circle surrounded by shapes, linked to form six sets of three shapes apiece. Can you complete the puzzle by placing each of the two-letter groups below, one per shape, so that every set of three (the central circle, plus the two matching shapes diagonally opposite one another) forms a six-letter word? Whichever pair of letters you place in the central circle will appear in the middle of every word.

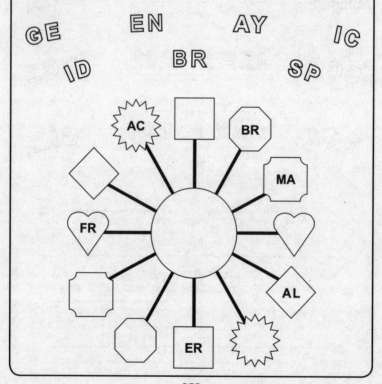

246

Keyword

On the face of it, this puzzle seems straightforward. Simply fill in the letters missing from words 1-8 and enter them into the numbered boxes, to reveal a hidden keyword.

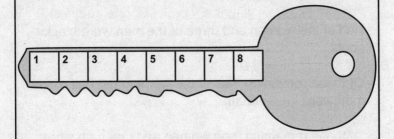

1	2	3	4	5	6	7	8

1 _ H O R N E _ _

2 _ X P E R T

3 G L O B _ L

4 M A _ G I N

5 M O N _ A Y

6 E N D E A _

7 P _ S T E R

8 I M _ U R E

247

Fractional Process

Fifteen people stood in line waiting for a bus.

The line comprised women, each standing in an odd-numbered position in line, and men, each standing in even-numbered positions.

Half of the women and three of the men wore black coats.

Of those remaining, half of the women and half of the men wore green coats.

Of those remaining, one woman and one man wore grey coats, and everyone else wore blue coats.

One woman and one man in each of the differently coloured coats carried an umbrella.

Of those remaining, one woman in a black coat, one woman in a green coat and one man in a black coat carried a bag.

How many men carried nothing?

248

Cut Out

Can you pair up shapes with the squares from which they were cut? Some may have been flipped over.

1

2

3

4

5

6

A

B

C

D

E

F

249

In at the Count

Precisely how many balls are in this picture?

Follow the Thread

These fishing lines have become tangled. Can you sort out which fish has been caught by each angler?

251

Fractions Wordsearch

```
H F D T J R M S H D J
T I L I D X E A J V B
X F X H E P L D S E B
I T O U O F M I R D W
S H T N I N M I R O G
C K V D U P T I X P I
O D F R L Z H H R E S
M T W E N T I E T H D
M G R D H T N E T Z X
O Z A T C O M P L E X
N H T H G I E F A L P
```

COMMON	NINTH
COMPLEX	ORDER
EIGHTH	SIMPLE
FIFTH	SIXTH
HALF	TENTH
HUNDREDTH	THIRD
MIXED	TWENTIETH

Sequence Conundrum

Which one of the lettered alternatives continues the sequence above?

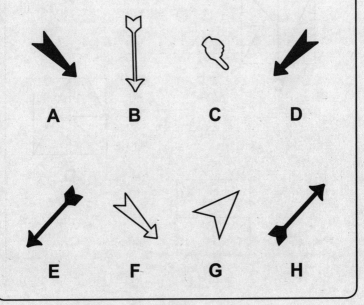

253

Odd One Out

Which is the odd one out – and why?

A

B

C

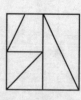

D

E

Sudoku

1		2	6				4	
	7	9		5	2		6	
		5	8					9
9	2			7		4		
8			2		6			7
		6		8			3	5
2					3	1		
	4		5	1		3	9	
	3				9	6		8

255

Wordfit

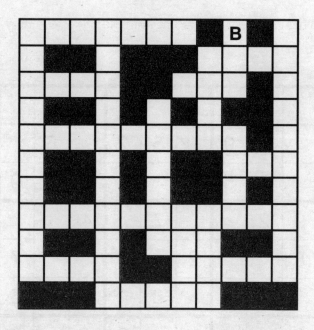

3 letters	TAME	9 letters
BAY	USED	REMAINDER
GAS		
HAY	**5 letters**	**10 letters**
OUT	METAL	AFTERWARDS
	NAKED	STRUCTURAL
4 letters		
GAME	**6 letters**	**11 letters**
HALT	ENDING	PREPARATION
HAZE		RECTANGULAR
ROLL	**7 letters**	
SOLO	AIRPORT	

Spot the Difference

Which of these is different from the rest – and how?

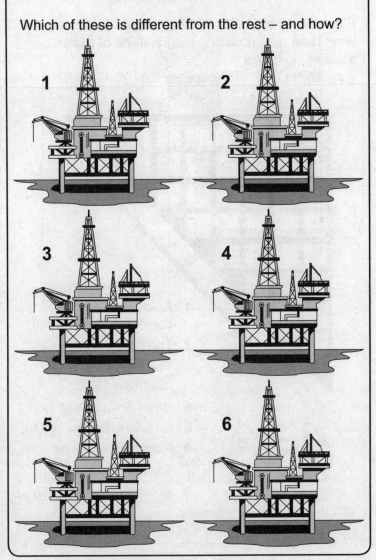

257

Character Assignation

Fill in the Across clues in this crossword in the normal way. Then read down the diagonal line of eight squares, to reveal:
A character from Shakespeare's *As You Like It*.

1 Anton ___, Austrian composer (1824–1896)
2 The USA's "Windy City"
3 The USA's "Sunflower State"
4 Hawaiian greeting
5 Be unsuccessful
6 Roman numeral for 7
7 Toward the centre
8 Roman numeral for 500

Character: ___ ___ ___ ___ ___ ___ ___ ___

258

Pyracross

Solve the clues on each level of the pyramid and reveal the word in the central column of bricks, a clue for which is: Ocean.

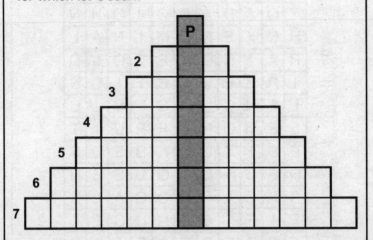

2 Hearing organ

3 Capital of Ghana

4 Country, capital La Paz

5 Paid driver

6 Florence ___, English nurse remembered for her work in the Crimean War

7 Former bass guitarist with the Beatles (4,9)

HIDDEN WORD: _____

259

Do It Yourself!

The listed words all appear in this crossword – you just need to blank out the unwanted squares...

T	O	A	D	A	D	O	J	O	H	N
H	O	X	E	N	O	M	I	N	A	L
R	A	I	N	O	Z	E	T	O	L	D
I	R	S	E	L	E	C	T	I	O	N
L	E	N	G	U	N	S	E	M	I	U
L	E	M	O	N	A	F	R	U	I	T
E	D	I	T	U	C	K	B	E	D	S
D	E	L	I	C	I	O	U	S	E	H
S	P	E	A	R	D	O	G	A	L	E
F	I	F	T	E	E	N	U	G	E	L
A	C	R	E	D	R	A	F	A	I	L

AXIS	FRUIT	NOMINAL
CIDER	GALE	NUTSHELL
DELICIOUS	HALO	RAIN
DOZEN	JITTERBUG	SAGA
EPIC	LEMON	SELECTION
FAIL	NEGOTIATE	THRILLED
FIFTEEN		TOAD

Letters Crossword

Each clue consists of letters in alphabetical order.
Rearrange these to form words, then fill the grid.

Across

3 DEEGL (5)
5 AABET (5)
7 RSTU (4)
9 EGHIORSTV (9)
11 CEEIIMNRS (9)
15 EEKP (4)
16 CEIMR (5)
17 BCKIR (5)

Down

1 AHLO (4)
2 ADER (4)
3 ELSS (4)
4 CIGHOT (6)
6 INPRTU (6)
8 DEIIRT (6)
10 EEIRVW (6)
12 CEKN (4)
13 IKPS (4)
14 EERV (4)

261

Around the Clock

Travel around the clock, one hour at a time, making twelve words all ending with the central letter. The letters to be placed in the empty squares are to be found in the segment clockwise of the number to be filled. We've completed one already, in order to get you off to a timely start…

Now take the central letter of every even-numbered word and rearrange these to form another, meaning: Go back to a previous state.

____ ____ ____ ____ ____ ____

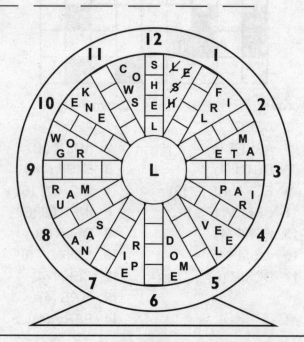

262

Around the Block

You won't need a starting block to get you under way, because it isn't a race! Just arrange the six-letter solutions to the clues into the six blocks around each clue number.

Write the answers in a clockwise or anticlockwise direction and you'll find that the last answer fits into the first; the main problem will be to decide in which square to put the first letter of each word...

1 Capital of South Dakota, USA

2 Slender, limited in width

3 Letters such as A, E, I, O, and U

4 Playing in opposition to

5 Make attractive or lovable

6 Acquaintance, ally

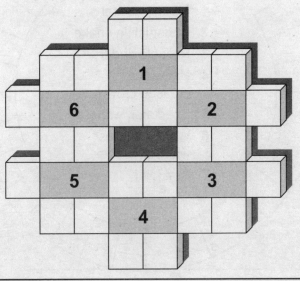

263

Roundword

Write the answer to each clue into the grid, working in a clockwise direction.

Every solution overlaps the next by either one, two, or three letters and each solution starts in its numbered section.

The solution to the final clue ends with the letter in the first square.

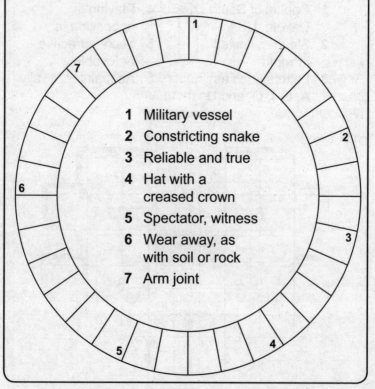

1 Military vessel
2 Constricting snake
3 Reliable and true
4 Hat with a creased crown
5 Spectator, witness
6 Wear away, as with soil or rock
7 Arm joint

264

Square Filler

The clues list the groups of adjacent blacked-out squares for each row and column, as you can see in this example:

Any adjacent blacked-out squares must have at least one white square between them and the next set of adjacent blacked-out squares.

Just follow the clues to fill in each row and column.

Dice Section

Printed onto every one of the six numbered dice are six letters (one per side), which can be rearranged to form the answer to each clue; however, some sides are invisible to you. Use the clues and write every answer into the grid. When correctly filled, the letters in the shaded squares, reading in the order 1 to 6, will spell out a US river.

1 Minor earthquake

2 Cower, cringe in submission

3 Deadly dangerous

4 Early calculating device

5 Reply

6 Former name of the capital of China

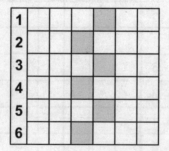

266

Pyramid Plus

Every brick in this pyramid contains a number which is the sum of the two numbers below it, so that F = A + B, etc.

Just work out the missing numbers!

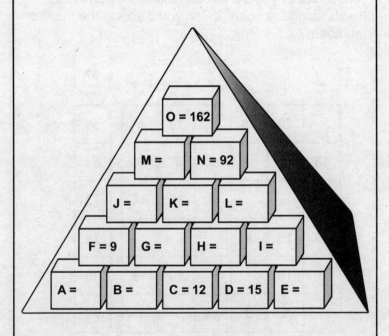

O = 162

M =   N = 92

J =   K =   L =

F = 9   G =   H =   I =

A =   B =   C = 12   D = 15   E =

267

Total Concentration

The blank squares below should be filled with whole numbers between 1 and 20 inclusive, any of which may occur more than once, or not at all.

The numbers in every horizontal row add up to the totals on the right, as do the two long diagonal lines; whilst those in every vertical column add up to the totals along the bottom. Can you discover the missing numbers?

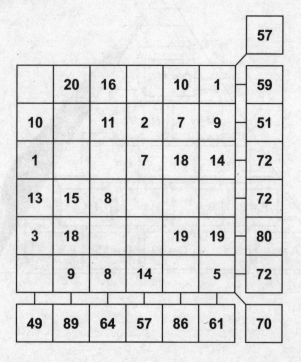

						57
	20	16		10	1	59
10		11	2	7	9	51
1			7	18	14	72
13	15	8				72
3	18			19	19	80
	9	8	14		5	72
49	89	64	57	86	61	70

268

Hexagony

Can you place the hexagons into the grid, so that where any hexagon touches another along a straight line, the contents of both triangles are the same? No rotation of any hexagon is allowed!

Number Fit

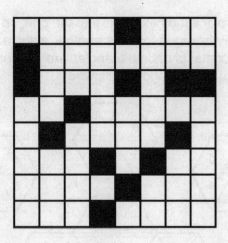

2 digits	550	5 digits
12	635	11878
13	741	12346
38	802	22038
47	833	37861
50		69483

	4 digits	
3 digits	2332	**7 digits**
176	2843	4527980
320	3766	
400	6952	
474	7234	
	9442	

Sudoku

2	7		1				3	
1				6	3	8		
	5				4	6		2
9	2	7	4	5				
8								1
				2	6	4	9	7
6		1	5				2	
		5	3	7				9
	9				8		4	3

271

Box Clever

When the box below is folded to form a cube, just one of the five options (A, B, C, D, or E) can be produced. Which?

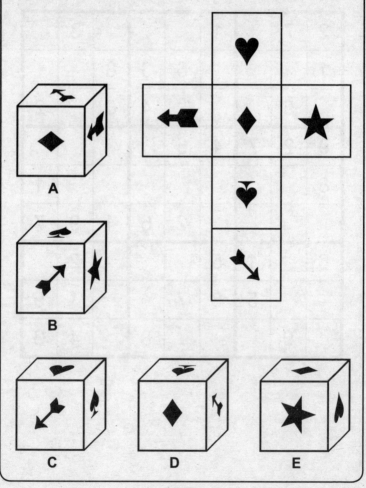

272

Sequence Conundrum

Which one of the lettered alternatives continues the sequence above?

A

B

C

D

273

Downwords

The solutions to the clues are all six-letter words, the letters for which are contained in the grid, at the rate of one per line and in the correct order from top to bottom. Every letter is used once only.

C	H	L	O	R	Y
A	B	I	L	O	U
E	E	O	P	R	X
D	K	N	P	R	U
A	C	I	L	O	R
E	E	H	H	N	Y

1 Grip tightly

C _____

2 Oriental tobacco pipe

H _____

3 Opulence

L _____

4 Shakespeare's "Fairy King"

O _____

5 Wavelet

R _____

6 Jamaican gangster

Y _____

Sum Circle

Fill the three empty circles with the symbols +, −, and x in some order to make a sum which totals the number in the centre.

Each symbol must be used once and calculations are made in the direction of travel (clockwise).

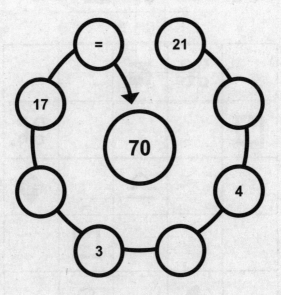

Shape Up

Each row and column of this grid should be filled with one of five different symbols, so that all five appear in that row or column.

Some are already in place – can you complete the grid?

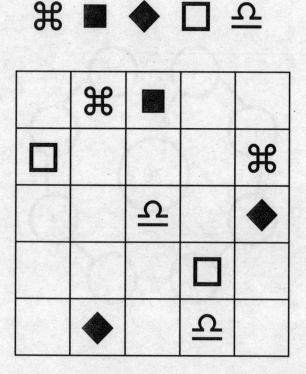

276

Eliminator

Every oval shape in this diagram contains a different letter of the alphabet from A to K inclusive. Use the clues to determine their locations. Reference in the clues to "due" means in any location along the same horizontal or vertical line.

1. A is next to and north of J, which is next to and east of H.

2. B is next to and north of G, which is next to and east of C.

3. D is due south of B, which is due west of I.

4. E is due north of H, which is next to and east of F.

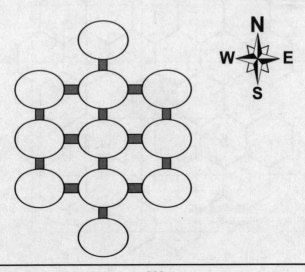

277

Hexafit

Can you place these six words into the hexagons? To fit them all in, some will have to be entered clockwise and others anticlockwise around the numbers.

Two letters have been placed already, which should give you a good start!

DENIAL   INSULT   LEADEN

MUSTER   NICKEL   POETIC

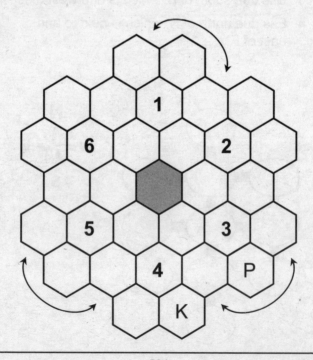

278

Stamp It Out!

Can you pair each of the stamps with its correct print?

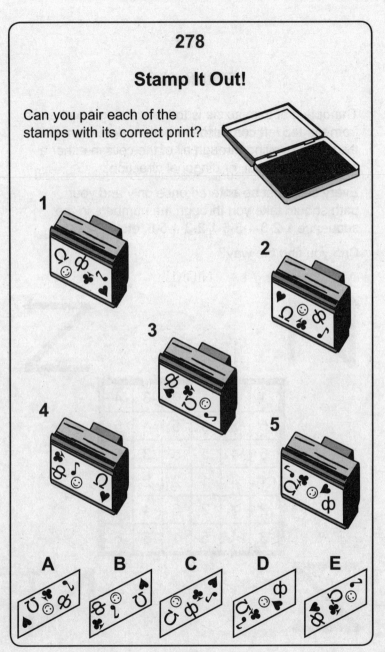

279

Pathfinder

The object of this puzzle is to trace a single path from the top left corner to the bottom right corner of the grid, travelling through all of the cells in either a horizontal, vertical, or diagonal direction.

Every cell must be entered once only and your path should take you through the numbers in the sequence 1-2-3-4-5-6-1-2-3-4-5-6, etc.

Can you find the way?

1	2	1	2	3	4
5	3	6	5	4	5
6	4	5	6	3	6
1	4	1	2	2	1
2	3	2	6	4	3
3	4	5	1	5	6

280

Memory Game

Study the picture below for 30 seconds and then turn to page 37.

This part of the test relates to the puzzle on page 87.
Which of the following have you just seen?

1

2

3

281

Shadows

Which of the shadows below is that of the snowman shown here?

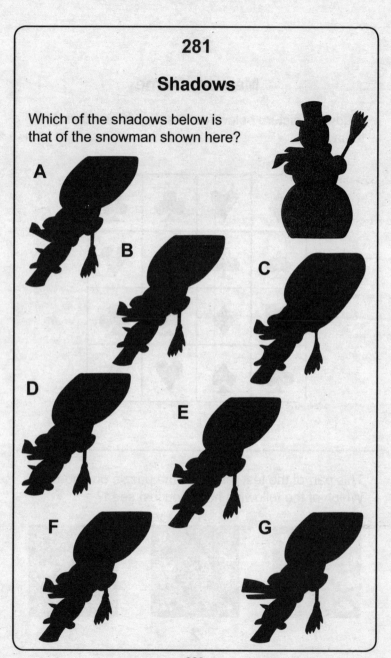

Jigsaw Puzzle

Which four shapes (two black and two white) can be fitted together to form the shape shown here?

The pieces may be rotated, but not flipped over.

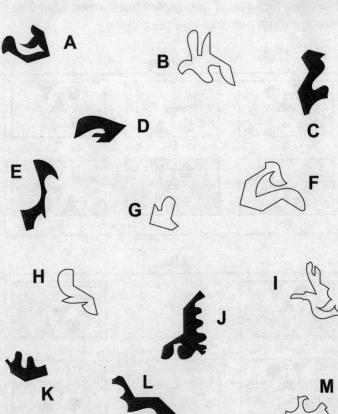

A

B

C

D

E

F

G

H

I

J

K

L

M

283

Buy-Buy

The Abstract Art Gallery has just sold a painting, after some deliberation by the customer, who took down each painting, turning it this way and that, before making a choice, and replacing five of the paintings haphazardly on the wall of the gallery.

Here are pictures of the display before and after the event. Which painting was purchased?

Before

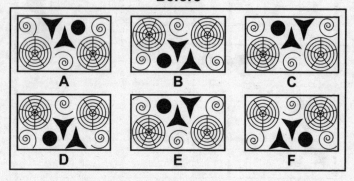

After

284

Sudoku

	6	2	5		7	1	9	
		1	6		4	2		
3				1				5
7			8	9	6			1
	1	9				8	4	
6			1	4	2			7
4				6				2
		3	9		1	4		
	7	6	4		8	3	5	

Word Ladder

Change one letter at a time (but not the position of any letter) to make a new word – and move from the word at the top of the ladder to the word at the bottom, using the exact number of rungs provided.

W I N D

M O A N

Treasure Hunt

The chart below gives directions to a hidden treasure behind the central black square in the grid.

Move the indicated number of spaces north, south, east, and west (e.g., 4N would mean four squares north) stopping at each square once only to arrive there.

At which square should you start?

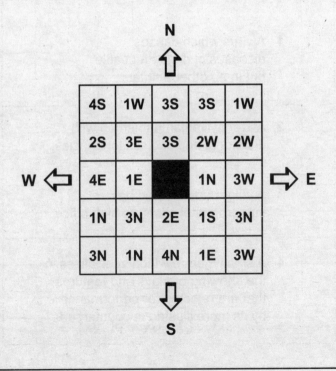

Wordpower

Which one of the four alternatives is the correct definition of the word shown below?

PARVENU

1 A virus which causes diseases in dogs and cattle but in no other animals

2 A Transylvanian nobleman with dictatorial and sadistic tendencies

3 A vulgar upstart who has inappropriately risen to high office

4 A small theatre which specializes in the showing of plays and features that are rejected for performance by its more illustrious counterparts

288

Maze

Can you trace your way through this maze, without taking your pencil from the paper?

289

Wordwheel

How many words of three or more letters can you make from those in the wheel, without using plurals, abbreviations, or proper nouns in just three minutes?

The central letter must appear once in every word and no letter in a section of the wheel may be used more than once.

There is at least one nine-letter word in the wheel.

Nine-letter word(s):

290

Tile Twister

Place the eight tiles into the puzzle grid so that all adjacent numbers on each tile match up. Any tile may be rotated, but none may be flipped over.

3	2
4	3

1	2
2	3

3	2
1	3

2	1
4	1

3	3
4	2

3	2
1	1

2	3
1	3

2	4
1	2

3	4				
2	1				

291

Bermuda Triangle

Travel through the "Bermuda Triangle" by visiting one room at a time to collect a letter from each. You can enter the outside passageway as often as you like, but can only visit each room once.

When you've completed your tour, the 15 letters (in order) will spell out a word.

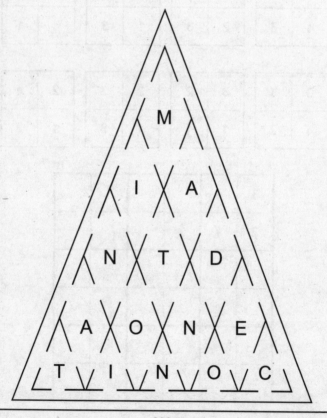

Shape Spotter

Which is the only shape to appear twice in the box below? You'll need a keen eye for this one, as some shapes overlap others!

293

Link Words

Fit different words into the central columns of the grid, so that each one links up with the words to either side, for example: table – lamp – shade.

When finished, read down the letters in the shaded squares to reveal another word, solving the clue below the grid.

BASE					LIGHTNING
MIDDLE					INDIES
MAIDEN					DROPPER
TYPE					LIFT
STONE					DUCK
SHORE					DANCING
COTTON					SACK
COCK					BOARD

Clue: Arthurian knight of the Round Table

Word: _____

Half and Half

Pair off these groups of three letters to make eight colours, each comprising six letters.

OON   SET   NGE   IGO

LOW   MAR   CER   VIO

ISE   YEL   RUS   ORA

PLE   IND   PUR   LET

_____   _____

_____   _____

_____   _____

_____   _____

295

Couplets

The picture is of a central circle surrounded by shapes, linked to form six sets of three shapes apiece. Can you complete the puzzle by placing each of the two-letter groups below, one per shape, so that every set of three (the central circle, plus the two matching shapes diagonally opposite one another) forms a six-letter word? Whichever pair of letters you place in the central circle will appear in the middle of every word.

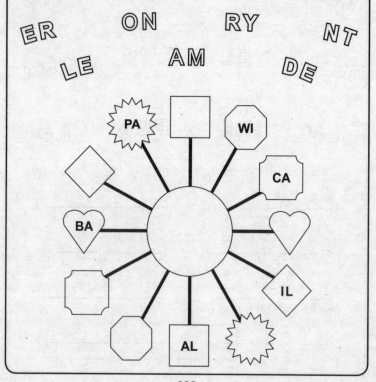

296

Keyword

On the face of it, this puzzle seems straightforward. Simply fill in the letters missing from words 1-8 and enter them into the numbered boxes, to reveal a hidden keyword.

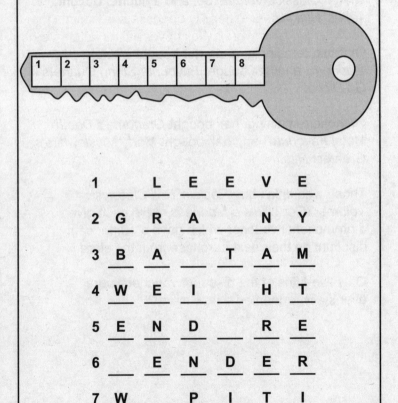

1	2	3	4	5	6	7	8

1 __ L E __ E V E

2 G R A __ N __ Y

3 B A __ T A M

4 W E I __ H T

5 E N D __ R E

6 __ E N D E R

7 W __ P __ I T I

8 U P W A __ D

Fractional Process

Sixteen people each bought a CD from a record store.

A quarter bought the latest rave compilation; *Rock 'n' Roll Classics Volume 36,* and a quarter bought *1980s' Hits 4U.*

Of those remaining, a quarter bought *Ukulele Madness*, and half bought *Favourite String Quartets Go Disco*.

Of those remaining, half bought *Grandma's Death Metal Favourites* and half bought *Morty Micklewhite's Greatest Hits.*

Those who didn't buy *Rock 'n' Roll Classics Volume 36* or *Ukulele Madness,* were each given a promotional voucher which gave a 10 per cent discount on their next purchase from the store.

Only two-fifths of the discount vouchers were eventually redeemed – how many?

298

Cut Out

Can you pair up shapes with the squares from which they were cut? Some may have been flipped over.

1

2

3

4

5

6

A

B

C

D

E

F

299

In at the Count

Precisely how many fish are in this picture?

300

Follow the Thread

These fishing lines have become tangled. Can you sort out which fish has been caught by each angler?

301

King Arthur Wordsearch

```
G W J K A N O L A V A
S G D K A R N O A J C
Y A A Z R R T I H T G
A Y F V B E O H M D A
J I O E O N H M U U R
L Q N V R N S T A R E
U I Z E I Y Z J U L T
C X O L S R O T C E H
A J R N K D E G O R E
N E X U E Q O M A R X
M X Q W R L T R H C G
```

ARTHUR	LAMORAK
AVALON	LIONEL
BORIS	LUCAN
DEGORE	MERLIN
GARETH	NIMUE
HECTOR	SAFER
KAY	UTHER

Sequence Conundrum

 ?

Which one of the lettered alternatives continues the sequence above?

A

B

C

D

E

F

Odd One Out

Which is the odd one out – and why?

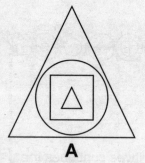

A

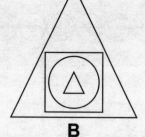

B

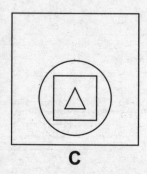

C

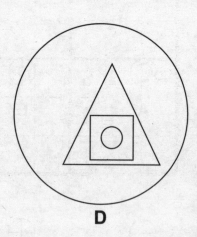

D

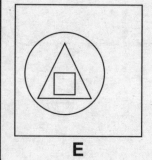

E

Sudoku

	1	6			8	5	3	
		5		1		2		
3		4	5			1		7
				2	9		5	8
	4						7	
5	6		7	3				
9		3			1	6		2
		2		6		8		
	8	1	4			7	9	

Wordfit

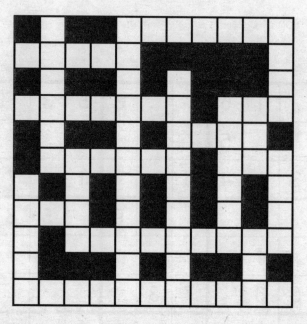

3 letter words
GOD
HAM
IMP
OWN
SHE

4 letter words
PINK
PIPE
PLEA
SAFE

5 letter words
LOGIC
PATCH

6 letter words
LADIES
SEIZED
SPHERE

7 letter words
PIMENTO
TETANUS

9 letter words
HOPEFULLY
KNOWLEDGE

11 letter words
COUNTRY-
    SIDE
THUNDER-
    BOLT

306

Spot the Difference

Which of these is different from the rest – and how?

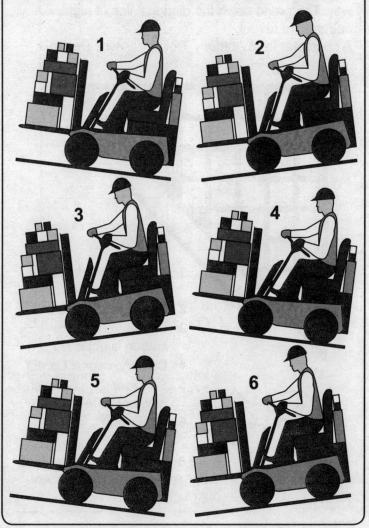

Character Assignation

Fill in the Across clues in this crossword in the normal way. Then read down the diagonal line of eight squares, to reveal:
A character from Anthony Trollope's *Alice Dugdale*.

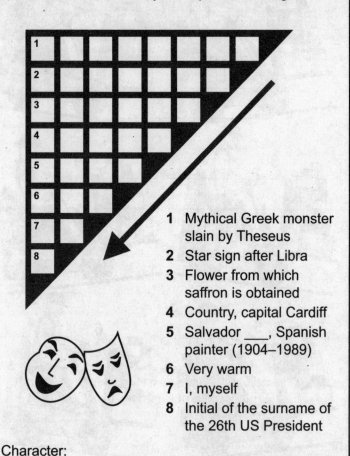

1 Mythical Greek monster slain by Theseus
2 Star sign after Libra
3 Flower from which saffron is obtained
4 Country, capital Cardiff
5 Salvador ___, Spanish painter (1904–1989)
6 Very warm
7 I, myself
8 Initial of the surname of the 26th US President

Character: ___ ___ ___ ___ ___ ___ ___ ___

308

Pyracross

Solve the clues on each level of the pyramid and reveal the word in the central column of bricks, a clue for which is: European country.

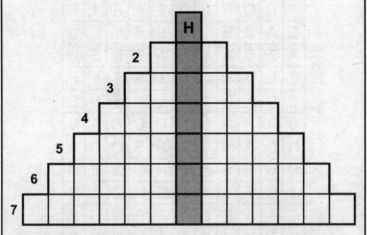

2 Hairy coat of an animal

3 Capital of Yemen

4 Capital of Thailand

5 Queen of England from 1558 to 1603

6 Weather forecasting

7 Popular child actress of the 1930s (7,6)

HIDDEN WORD: _____

Do It Yourself!

The listed words all appear in this crossword – you just need to blank out the unwanted squares…

A	D	O	P	E	R	B	A	S	I	S
G	A	Z	E	L	L	E	B	I	C	U
A	Z	C	A	N	E	W	S	D	E	R
B	E	A	R	D	N	I	S	E	L	F
C	U	P	E	A	T	L	A	S	H	E
C	A	P	S	U	N	D	C	H	A	D
H	D	A	N	G	L	E	S	O	D	A
O	U	R	S	H	E	R	O	W	E	R
I	C	E	D	T	E	E	M	O	A	S
C	A	N	E	E	X	P	E	N	S	E
E	N	T	E	R	E	D	N	E	Y	E

ANGLE	CHOICE	HAD
APPARENT	DAUGHTER	OMEN
ATLAS	DAZE	OUR
BASIS	EASY	PEAR
BEARD	ELF	ROWER
BEWILDER	ENTER	SIDESHOW
CAP	EXPENSE	SURFED
	GAZELLE	

310

Letters Crossword

Each clue consists of letters in alphabetical order. Rearrange these to form words, then fill the grid.

Across

3 AABMS (5)
5 EINNU (5)
6 DDEGO (5)
8 HENW (4)
10 ACEN (4)
12 ACKS (4)
15 EELR (4)
17 AEESV (5)
18 AADNP (5)
19 EJLLY (5)

Down

1 ADELT (5)
2 KNNOW (5)
3 DEIS (4)
4 BGOSU (5)
7 CENO (4)
9 EEHR (4)
11 ACERZ (5)
13 AELNO (5)
14 AAKKY (5)
16 EPSY (4)

311

Around the Clock

Travel around the clock, one hour at a time, making twelve words all ending with the central letter. The letters to be placed in the empty squares are to be found in the segment clockwise of the number to be filled. We've completed one already, in order to get you off to a timely start…

Now take the central letter of every even-numbered word and rearrange these to form another, meaning: Request forcefully.

___ ___ ___ ___ ___ ___

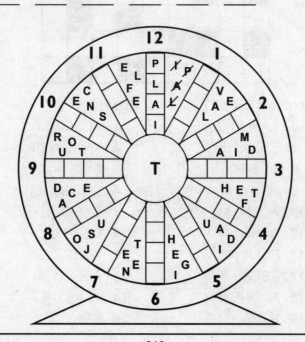

Around the Block

You won't need a starting block to get you under way, because it isn't a race! Just arrange the six-letter solutions to the clues into the six blocks around each clue number.

Write the answers in a clockwise or anticlockwise direction and you'll find that the last answer fits into the first; the main problem will be to decide in which square to put the first letter of each word…

1 Plot of land adjoining a house

2 Country, capital Amman

3 Grasp hastily or eagerly

4 Small, air-breathing arthropod

5 Deep, narrow valley

6 US state, capital Carson City

313

Roundword

Write the answer to each clue into the grid, working in a clockwise direction.

Every solution overlaps the next by either one, two, or three letters and each solution starts in its numbered section.

The solution to the final clue ends with the letter in the first square.

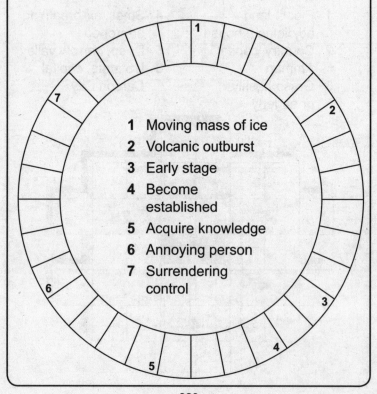

1 Moving mass of ice
2 Volcanic outburst
3 Early stage
4 Become established
5 Acquire knowledge
6 Annoying person
7 Surrendering control

314

Square Filler

The clues list the groups of adjacent blacked-out squares for each row and column, as you can see in this example:

Any adjacent blacked-out squares must have at least one white square between them and the next set of adjacent blacked-out squares.

Just follow the clues to fill in each row and column.

315

Dice Section

Printed onto every one of the six numbered dice are six letters (one per side), which can be rearranged to form the answer to each clue; however, some sides are invisible to you. Use the clues and write every answer into the grid. When correctly filled, the letters in the shaded squares, reading in the order 1 to 6, will spell out a planet.

1 Ill-treated

2 Brisk, zippy

3 Electromagnetic particle

4 Relating to horses

5 Overwhelming fear

6 Teacher, trusted counsellor

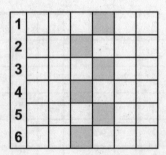

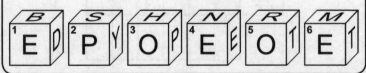

316

Pyramid Plus

Every brick in this pyramid contains a number which is the sum of the two numbers below it, so that F = A + B, etc.

Just work out the missing numbers!

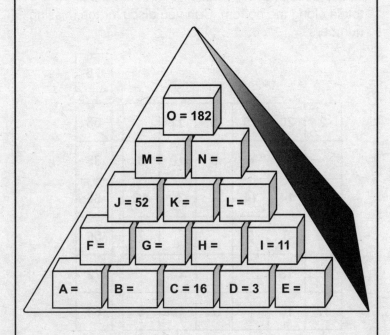

317

Total Concentration

The blank squares below should be filled with whole numbers between 1 and 20 inclusive, any of which may occur more than once, or not at all.

The numbers in every horizontal row add up to the totals on the right, as do the two long diagonal lines; whilst those in every vertical column add up to the totals along the bottom. Can you discover the missing numbers?

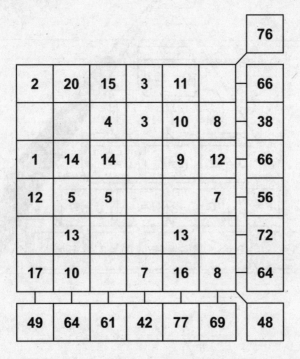

						76
2	20	15	3	11		66
		4	3	10	8	38
1	14	14		9	12	66
12	5	5			7	56
	13			13		72
17	10		7	16	8	64
49	64	61	42	77	69	48

318

Hexagony

Can you place the hexagons into the grid, so that where any hexagon touches another along a straight line, the contents of both triangles are the same? No rotation of any hexagon is allowed!

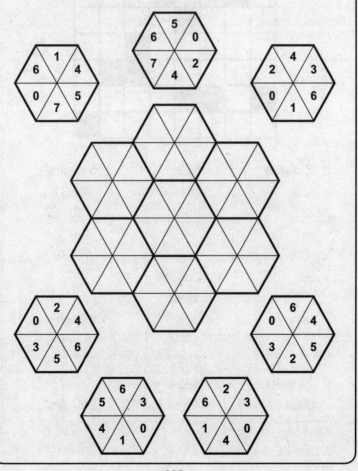

Number Fit

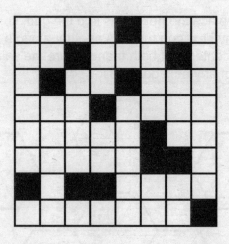

2 digits	562	5 digits
15	756	20831
33	938	38017
47		48930
60		50238
65	**4 digits**	
73	1892	
87	2257	**6 digits**
	3764	540945
	5322	
3 digits	5834	
143		**7 digits**
277		1789135
415		2977034

320

Sudoku

	1			9	5			
		9				6	2	7
8	4				2			5
		5		2	1	4	7	
	9		8		7		6	
	8	1	4	3		2		
5			6				8	3
1	6	3				9		
			2	4			1	

321

Box Clever

When the box below is folded to form a cube, just one of the five options (A, B, C, D, or E) can be produced. Which?

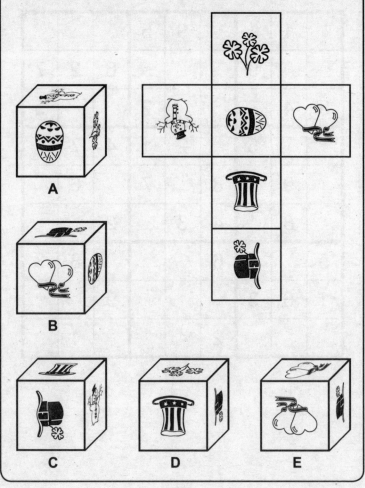

A

B

C

D

E

322

Sequence Conundrum

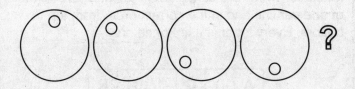

Which one of the lettered alternatives continues the sequence above?

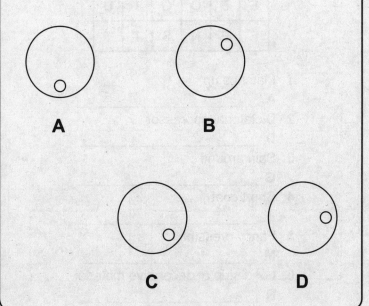

A

B

C

D

323

Downwords

The solutions to the clues are all six-letter words, the letters for which are contained in the grid, at the rate of one per line and in the correct order from top to bottom. Every letter is used once only.

A	D	G	J	M	R
A	A	E	I	G	Y
B	C	R	R	S	S
A	B	E	K	P	Q
E	E	O	O	T	U
E	E	N	S	T	T

1 Matches up
   A _____

2 Dictatorial oppressor
   D _____

3 Spin around
   G _____

4 Short coat
   J _____

5 Fancy-dress ball
   M _____

6 Long strip of decorative material
   R _____

324

Sum Circle

Fill the three empty circles with the symbols +, −, and x in some order to make a sum which totals the number in the centre.

Each symbol must be used once and calculations are made in the direction of travel (clockwise).

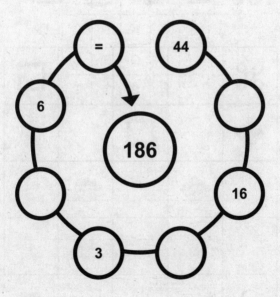

325

Shape Up

Each row and column of this grid should be filled with one of five different symbols, so that all five appear in that row or column.

Some are already in place – can you complete the grid?

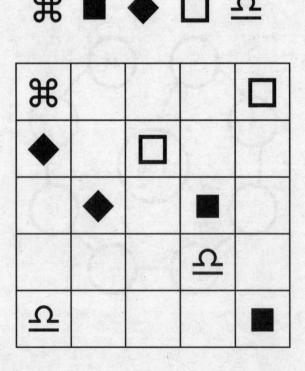

326

Eliminator

Every oval shape in this diagram contains a different letter of the alphabet from A to K inclusive. Use the clues to determine their locations. Reference in the clues to "due" means in any location along the same horizontal or vertical line.

1   A is next to and west of B, which is further south than F.
2   B is due north of C, which is next to and west of J.
3   D is further north than I, which is further west than G.
4   E is due south of H, which is next to and east of K.
5   F is due east of the letter which is due south of G.

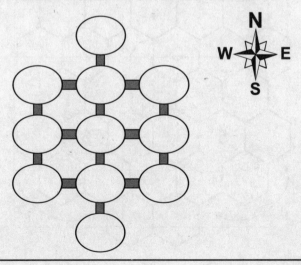

Hexafit

Can you place these six words into the hexagons? To fit them all in, some will have to be entered clockwise and others anticlockwise around the numbers.

Two letters have been placed already, which should give you a good start!

CASKET   CYGNET   FIXATE

GALAXY   STRIFE   TRASHY

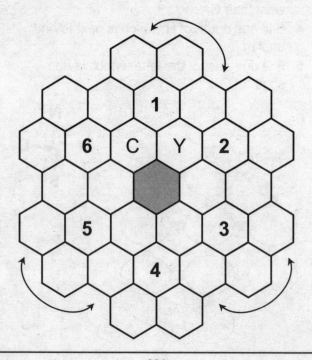

Stamp It Out!

Can you pair each of the stamps with its correct print?

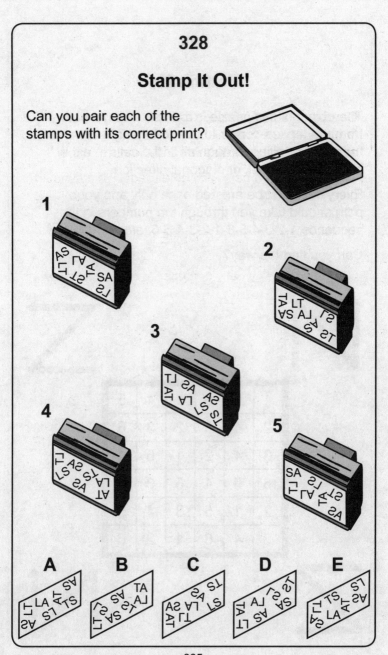

1

2

3

4

5

A **B** **C** **D** **E**

Pathfinder

The object of this puzzle is to trace a single path from the top left corner to the bottom right corner of the grid, travelling through all of the cells in either a horizontal, vertical, or diagonal direction.

Every cell must be entered once only and your path should take you through the numbers in the sequence 1-2-3-4-5-6-1-2-3-4-5-6, etc.

Can you find the way?

1	5	6	1	4	5
2	4	3	2	3	6
3	4	2	1	6	1
6	5	4	5	3	2
2	1	5	3	4	5
3	4	6	1	2	6

330

Memory Game

Study the picture below for 30 seconds and then turn to page 137.

This part of the test relates to the puzzle on page 187. Which of the following have you just seen?

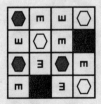

1

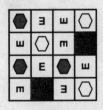

2

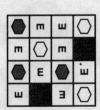

3

331

Shadows

Which of the shadows below is that of the anchor shown here?

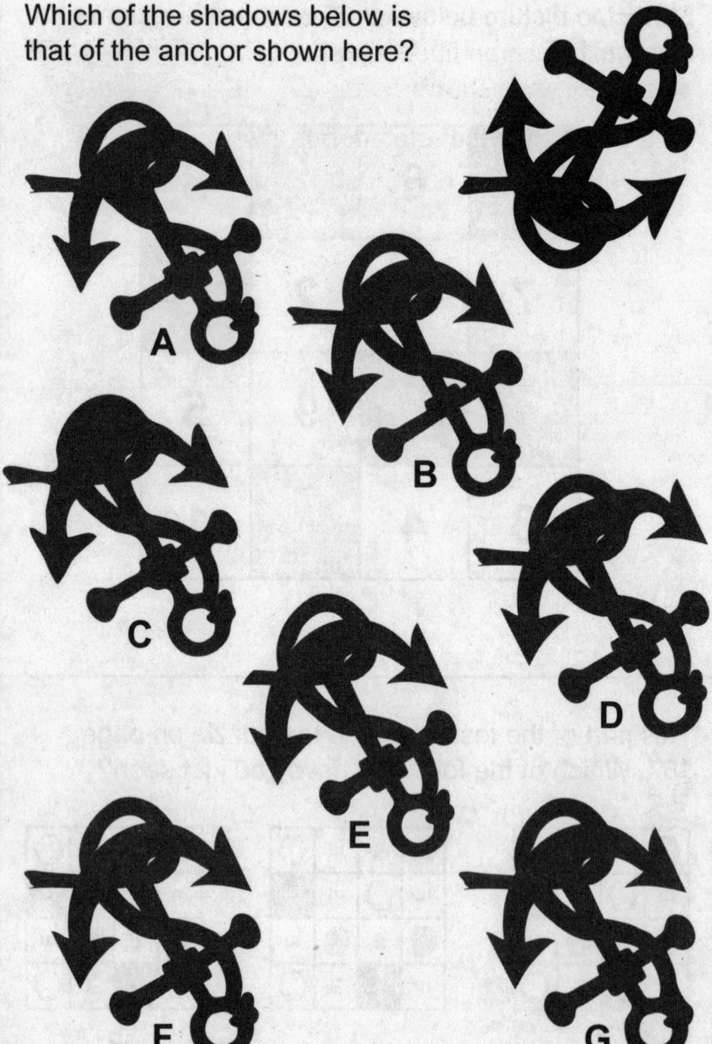

332

Jigsaw Puzzle

Which four shapes (two black and two white) can be fitted together to form the shape shown here?

The pieces may be rotated, but not flipped over.

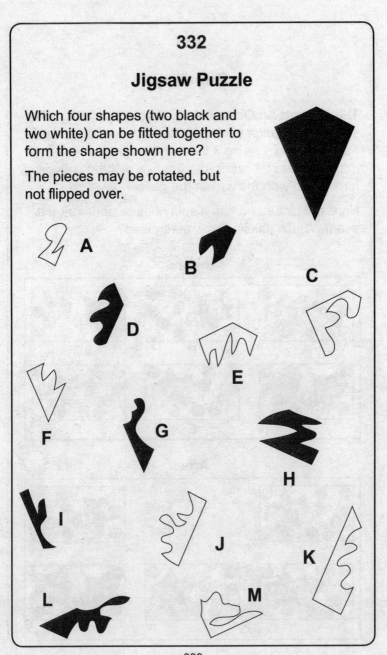

A

B

C

D

E

F

G

H

I

J

K

L

M

333

Buy-Buy

The Abstract Art Gallery has just sold a painting, after some deliberation by the customer, who took down each painting, turning it this way and that, before making a choice, and replacing five of the paintings haphazardly on the wall of the gallery.

Here are pictures of the display before and after the event. Which painting was purchased?

Before

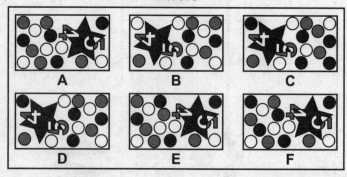

After

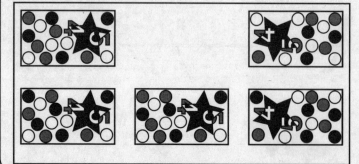

Sudoku

	2		7	8	9			
	4			1		5	2	9
	6		4		5			
2			1		6	7		
8	5						3	1
		6	5		8			2
			3		7		1	
9	7	3		6			4	
			9	4	2		7	

Word Ladder

Change one letter at a time (but not the position of any letter) to make a new word – and move from the word at the top of the ladder to the word at the bottom, using the exact number of rungs provided.

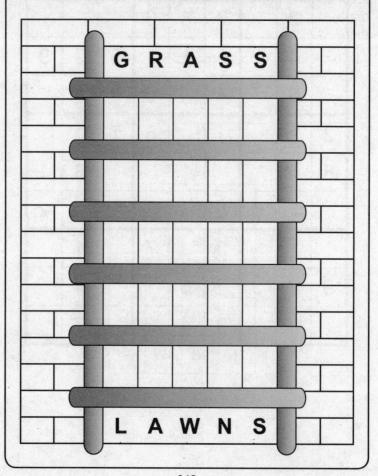

GRASS

LAWNS

336

Treasure Hunt

The chart below gives directions to a hidden treasure behind the central black square in the grid.

Move the indicated number of spaces north, south, east, and west (e.g., 4N would mean four squares north) stopping at each square once only to arrive there.

At which square should you start?

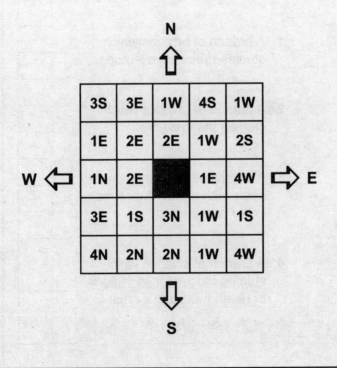

Wordpower

Which one of the four alternatives is the correct definition of the word shown below?

URANOLOGY

1 A branch of physics which studies radioactive isotopes

2 A branch of physics which studies the universe

3 A branch of medicine which deals with urinary functions in the human body

4 A branch of science which studies processes in regions beneath the Earth's crust

338

Maze

Can you trace your way through this maze, without taking your pencil from the paper?

339

Wordwheel

How many words of three or more letters can you make from those in the wheel, without using plurals, abbreviations, or proper nouns in just three minutes?

The central letter must appear once in every word and no letter in a section of the wheel may be used more than once.

There is at least one nine-letter word in the wheel.

Nine-letter word(s):

340

Tile Twister

Place the eight tiles into the puzzle grid so that all adjacent numbers on each tile match up. Any tile may be rotated, but none may be flipped over.

1	3
4	1

2	1
1	4

4	1
3	1

2	2
4	3

4	1
2	2

4	4
1	3

2	1
3	4

3	4
4	1

2	1				
1	1				

341

Bermuda Triangle

Travel through the "Bermuda Triangle" by visiting one room at a time to collect a letter from each. You can enter the outside passageway as often as you like, but can only visit each room once.

When you've completed your tour, the 15 letters (in order) will spell out a word.

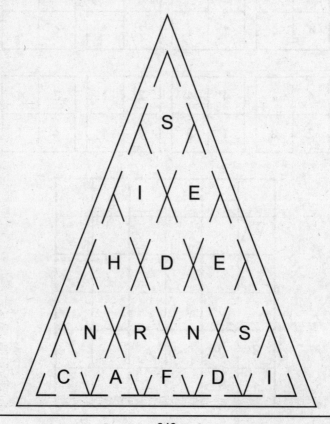

342

Shape Spotter

Which is the only shape to appear twice in the box below? You'll need a keen eye for this one, as some shapes overlap others!

343

Link Words

Fit different words into the central columns of the grid, so that each one links up with the words to either side, for example: table – lamp – shade.

When finished, read down the letters in the shaded squares to reveal another word, solving the clue below the grid.

SECOND						SOME
QUICK						STONE
GEORGE						BABY
GOLF						HORSE
WIDE						HOUSE
FOR						LASTING
FOOT						BROTHER
FUN						HEARING

Clue: Find out

Word: _____

Half and Half

Pair off these groups of three letters to make eight minerals, metals, or gems, each comprising six letters.

ENA   CON   PER   RAD

VER   COP   GAR   GYP

SUM   IUM   GAL   ZIR

PER   SIL   NET   JAS

_____   _____

_____   _____

_____   _____

_____   _____

345

Couplets

The picture is of a central circle surrounded by shapes, linked to form six sets of three shapes apiece. Can you complete the puzzle by placing each of the two-letter groups below, one per shape, so that every set of three (the central circle, plus the two matching shapes diagonally opposite one another) forms a six-letter word? Whichever pair of letters you place in the central circle will appear in the middle of every word.

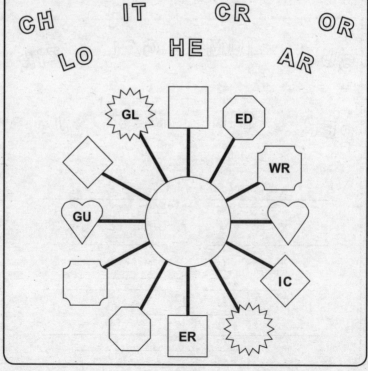

CH IT CR OR

LO HE AR

GL ED WR GU IC ER

346

Keyword

On the face of it, this puzzle seems straightforward. Simply fill in the letters missing from words 1-8 and enter them into the numbered boxes, to reveal a hidden keyword.

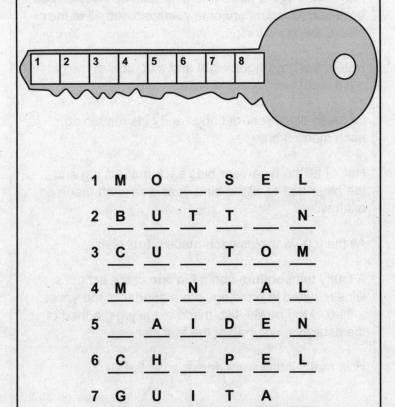

1	2	3	4	5	6	7	8

1 M O _ S E L
2 B U T T _ N
3 C U _ T O M
4 M _ N I A L
5 _ A I D E N
6 C H _ P E L
7 G U I T A _
8 L A R _ N X

347

Fractional Process

Eighteen children (half are boys and half are girls) made items from clay in craft class.

Two-thirds of the boys are eight years old, as are four-ninths of the girls. Of the remaining children, two boys and four girls are nine years old and all of the others are aged ten.

Half of the boys aged eight and a quarter of the girls aged eight each made a vase.

Of those eight-year-old boys and girls remaining, each made a bowl.

Half of all the nine-year-olds each made a jug and the other half of all the nine-year-olds each made an ashtray.

All the ten-year-olds each made a fruit dish.

A faulty temperature-control in one of the school's kilns resulted in breakages to a quarter of the vases, a third of the bowls, two-thirds of the jugs, a third of the ashtrays, and half of the fruit dishes.

How many items were damaged in the kiln?

Cut Out

Can you pair up shapes with the squares from which they were cut? Some may have been flipped over.

 1

 2

 3

 **4**

 5

 6

 A

 B

 C

 D

 E

 F

349

In at the Count

Precisely how many apples are in this picture?

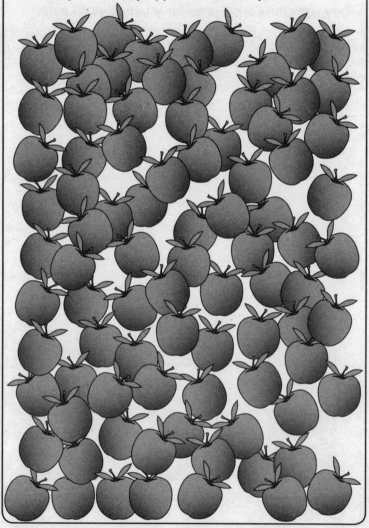

350

Follow the Thread

These fishing lines have become tangled. Can you sort out which fish has been caught by each angler?

351

Furniture Wordsearch

```
E B O R D R A W S E D
N W K E Z G S C C I D
V E S P H A O O S O H
B K V J U M U H F I S
S U T O M C W B G A C
E A R O H A S H T K R
E P D E S H C M C J E
T E I H A H Z O B P E
T T E A A U L U F V N
E R R I N C T S E H C
S O R F G O U K V K P
```

BUREAU	HIGH CHAIR
CHEST	OVEN
CLOCK	PIANO
COMMODE	SCREEN
COUCH	SETTEE
DESK	SOFA
DISHWASHER	WARDROBE

352

Sequence Conundrum

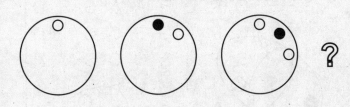

Which one of the lettered alternatives continues the sequence above?

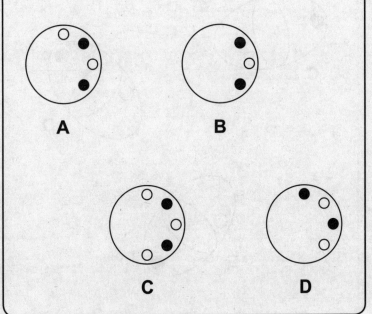

Odd One Out

Which is the odd one out – and why?

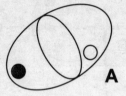

A

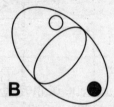

B

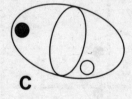

C

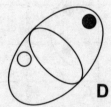

D

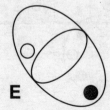

E

354

Sudoku

			2		9			3
4	7	9		1				2
			6	5	7			4
	4		9		5	3		
8	1						5	9
		6	1		3		4	
6			7	2	4			
2				3		8	7	6
1			8		6			

355

Wordfit

3 letters
ERA
FAR
NET
WEB

4 letters
BABY
BASS
HERB
KNEW
NEWT
PACT

REAP
SANG
SOWN
TUFT
YETI

5 letters
NIECE

6 letters
NECTAR
TOYING

7 letters
BARONET
ROSETTE

10 letters
REORDERING

11 letters
ADOLESCENCE
HUCKLEBERRY

356

Spot the Difference

Which of these is different from the rest – and how?

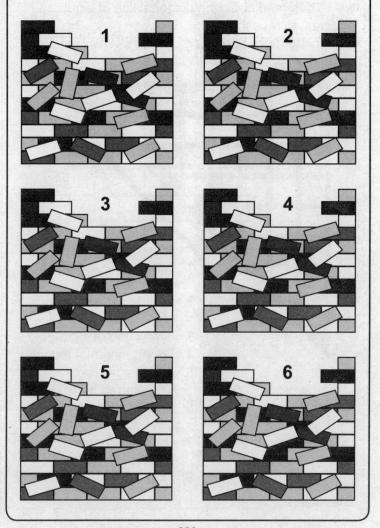

357

Character Assignation

Fill in the Across clues in this crossword in the normal way. Then read down the diagonal line of eight squares, to reveal:
A character from Shakespeare's *All's Well That Ends Well*.

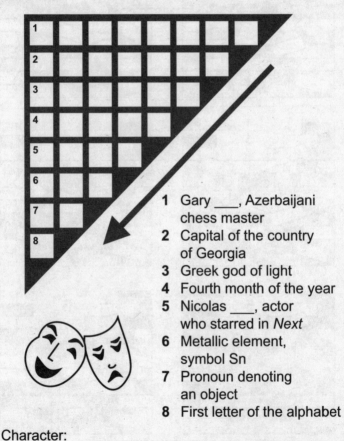

1 Gary ___, Azerbaijani chess master
2 Capital of the country of Georgia
3 Greek god of light
4 Fourth month of the year
5 Nicolas ___, actor who starred in *Next*
6 Metallic element, symbol Sn
7 Pronoun denoting an object
8 First letter of the alphabet

Character: __ __ __ __ __ __ __ __

358

Pyracross

Solve the clues on each level of the pyramid and reveal the word in the central column of bricks, a clue for which is: Venetian canal boat.

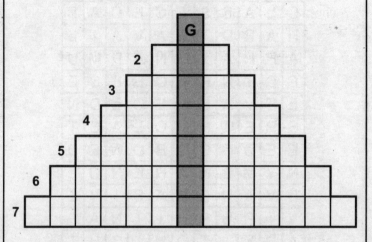

2 Canine animal

3 Country, capital Nairobi

4 Country, capital Chişinău

5 Body of water into which the Canadian rivers Nelson and Churchill flow (6,3)

6 Capital of Malaysia until 2005 (5,6)

7 Desert creature with two humps (8,5)

HIDDEN WORD: _____

Do It Yourself!

The listed words all appear in this crossword – you just need to blank out the unwanted squares…

C	L	A	S	S	I	C	E	C	A	F
H	A	R	D	T	E	A	V	A	I	L
A	R	R	A	I	G	N	A	R	M	U
P	D	I	N	R	R	O	B	E	S	E
E	E	V	A	S	E	E	O	L	D	N
G	R	E	W	N	G	O	L	A	S	T
E	E	G	G	C	O	B	D	W	E	D
N	Y	M	P	H	A	R	E	N	O	L
E	V	A	N	E	V	A	S	I	V	E
V	I	R	U	S	B	I	T	N	A	F
A	R	K	I	T	O	N	I	G	H	T

ARRAIGN	CHEST	LEFT
ARRIVE	CLASSIC	MARK
AVAIL	COB	NYMPH
AWNING	EGO	OBESE
BRAIN	EVASIVE	SEE
CANOE	FLUENT	STIRS
CARE	GENEVA	TONIGHT
CHAP	GREW	VIRUS
	LAST	

360

Letters Crossword

Each clue consists of letters in alphabetical order.
Rearrange these to form words, then fill the grid.

Across
- **1** ABIT (4)
- **4** DEIL (4)
- **7** AMN (3)
- **9** EPRSS (5)
- **10** ACR (3)
- **11** AHS (3)
- **12** CIOPT (5)
- **13** AHM (3)
- **14** EIL (3)
- **15** AINOP (5)
- **17** ELT (3)
- **18** DGRU (4)
- **19** HSTU (4)

Down
- **1** ABCDEHKLO (9)
- **2** IMMOPPRTU (9)
- **3** ART (3)
- **5** CDHHILOST (9)
- **6** EIIMNOSSS (9)
- **8** AELNRTU (7)
- **16** ENT (3)

361

Around the Clock

Travel around the clock, one hour at a time, making twelve words all ending with the central letter. The letters to be placed in the empty squares are to be found in the segment clockwise of the number to be filled. We've completed one already, in order to get you off to a timely start…

Now take the central letter of every even-numbered word and rearrange these to form another, meaning: Vocation, occupation.

___ ___ ___ ___ ___ ___

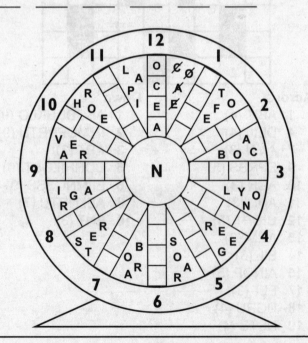

362

Around the Block

You won't need a starting block to get you under way, because it isn't a race! Just arrange the six-letter solutions to the clues into the six blocks around each clue number.

Write the answers in a clockwise or anticlockwise direction and you'll find that the last answer fits into the first; the main problem will be to decide in which square to put the first letter of each word…

1 Orange root vegetable
2 Excuse, forgive
3 Capital of England

4 Country, capital Oslo
5 Noontime
6 Reflect

363

Roundword

Write the answer to each clue into the grid, working in a clockwise direction.

Every solution overlaps the next by either one, two, or three letters and each solution starts in its numbered section.

The solution to the final clue ends with the letter in the first square.

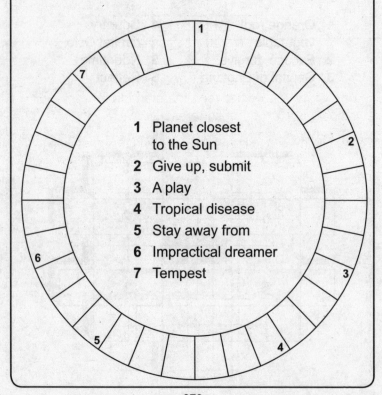

1 Planet closest to the Sun
2 Give up, submit
3 A play
4 Tropical disease
5 Stay away from
6 Impractical dreamer
7 Tempest

364

Square Filler

The clues list the groups of adjacent blacked-out squares for each row and column, as you can see in this example:

Any adjacent blacked-out squares must have at least one white square between them and the next set of adjacent blacked-out squares.

Just follow the clues to fill in each row and column.

2 1 1						
2 2						
1 4						
2 3						
3 2						
1 2						
	5	2 3	1 1	1 2	5	6

365

Dice Section

Printed onto every one of the six numbered dice are six letters (one per side), which can be rearranged to form the answer to each clue; however, some sides are invisible to you. Use the clues and write every answer into the grid. When correctly filled, the letters in the shaded squares, reading in the order 1 to 6, will spell out a famous Rocky Mountains peak.

1 Mythical tale

2 Old Western drinking place

3 Irrational fear

4 Acid found in vinegar

5 Containing iron

6 Shrivel up, as with loss of moisture

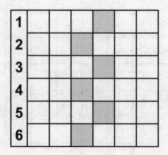

366

Pyramid Plus

Every brick in this pyramid contains a number which is the sum of the two numbers below it, so that F = A + B, etc.

Just work out the missing numbers!

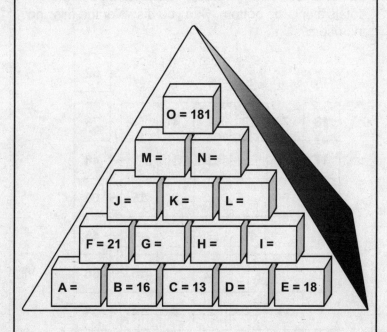

Total Concentration

The blank squares below should be filled with whole numbers between 1 and 20 inclusive, any of which may occur more than once, or not at all.

The numbers in every horizontal row add up to the totals on the right, as do the two long diagonal lines; whilst those in every vertical column add up to the totals along the bottom. Can you discover the missing numbers?

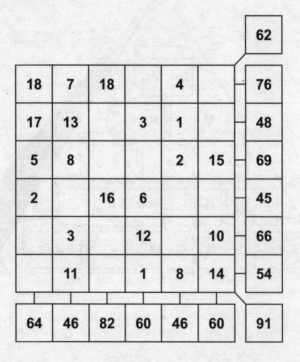

						62
18	7	18		4		76
17	13		3	1		48
5	8			2	15	69
2		16	6			45
	3		12		10	66
	11		1	8	14	54
64	46	82	60	46	60	91

Hexagony

Can you place the hexagons into the grid, so that where any hexagon touches another along a straight line, the contents of both triangles are the same? No rotation of any hexagon is allowed!

369

Number Fit

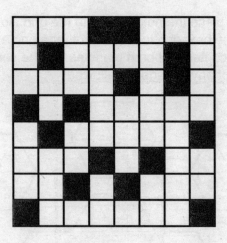

2 digits	354	5 digits
10	376	11598
44	532	47974
45	807	94357
57	829	94409
73	976	
85		
93		**6 digits**
	4 digits	223559
3 digits	2724	
199	6197	
239	6568	
318	7717	

Sudoku

4		8			9	1		7
		2			4		6	
5			3	8	6			4
	9		6			7		
2		6				4		8
		3			5		2	
1			7	2	3			6
	7		5			3		
3		5	4			9		1

371

Box Clever

When the box below is folded to form a cube, just one of the five options (A, B, C, D, or E) can be produced. Which?

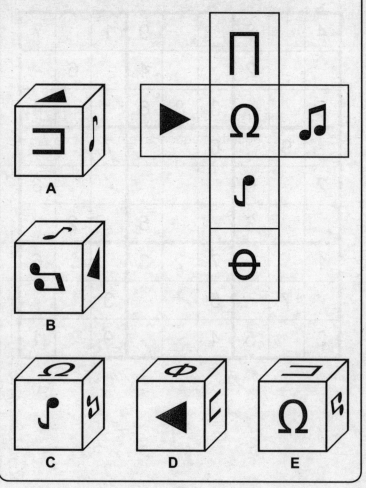

A

B

C

D

E

372

Sequence Conundrum

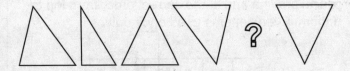

Which one of the lettered alternatives should replace the question mark in the sequence above?

A   B

C   D

373

Downwords

The solutions to the clues are all six-letter words, the letters for which are contained in the grid, at the rate of one per line and in the correct order from top to bottom. Every letter is used once only.

I	M	P	T	V	Z
A	E	L	O	T	U
A	D	H	L	T	U
G	I	L	R	R	U
A	A	A	A	I	R
C	C	E	L	N	R

1 Slanted letter

I _____

2 Ripe, aged

M _____

3 More than one

P _____

4 Capital of Iran

T _____

5 Crude, uncouth

V _____

6 Group of 12 constellations

Z _____

374

Sum Circle

Fill the three empty circles with the symbols +, −, and x in some order to make a sum which totals the number in the centre.

Each symbol must be used once and calculations are made in the direction of travel (clockwise).

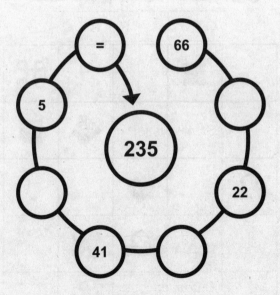

Shape Up

Each row and column of this grid should be filled with one of five different symbols, so that all five appear in that row or column.

Some are already in place – can you complete the grid?

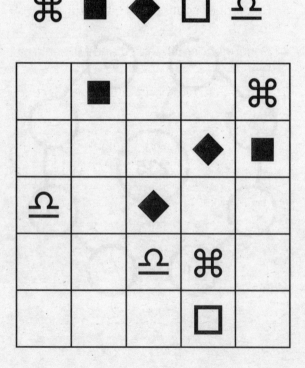

376

Eliminator

Every oval shape in this diagram contains a different letter of the alphabet from A to K inclusive. Use the clues to determine their locations. Reference in the clues to "due" means in any location along the same horizontal or vertical line.

1. A is next to and due west of D.

2. D is due north of I, which is next to and west of F.

3. E is further south than H, but further north than J.

4. G is further south than J and further east than K.

5. H is next to and north of C, which is due east of B.

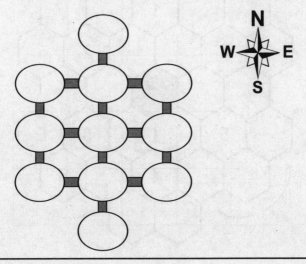

377

Hexafit

Can you place these six words into the hexagons? To fit them all in, some will have to be entered clockwise and others anticlockwise around the numbers.

Two letters have been placed already, which should give you a good start!

LITTLE   NEREID   RHESUS

SUPPER   TENANT   THRILL

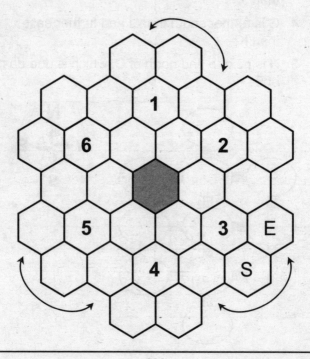

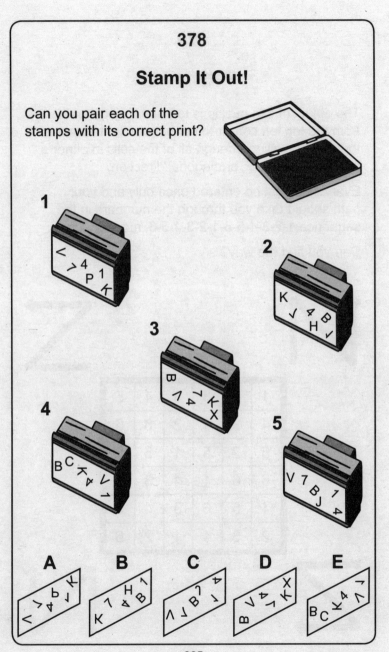

378

Stamp It Out!

Can you pair each of the stamps with its correct print?

Pathfinder

The object of this puzzle is to trace a single path from the top left corner to the bottom right corner of the grid, travelling through all of the cells in either a horizontal, vertical, or diagonal direction.

Every cell must be entered once only and your path should take you through the numbers in the sequence 1-2-3-4-5-6-1-2-3-4-5-6, etc.

Can you find the way?

1	2	3	3	4	5
4	3	4	2	6	6
5	2	5	1	5	1
6	6	1	4	3	2
1	5	6	3	4	5
2	3	4	1	2	6

Memory Game

Study the picture below for 30 seconds and then turn to page 187.

This part of the test relates to the puzzle on page 237. Which of the following have you just seen?

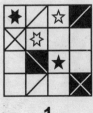

1

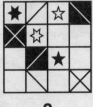

2

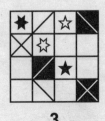

3

381

Shadows

Which of the shadows below is that of the witch shown here?

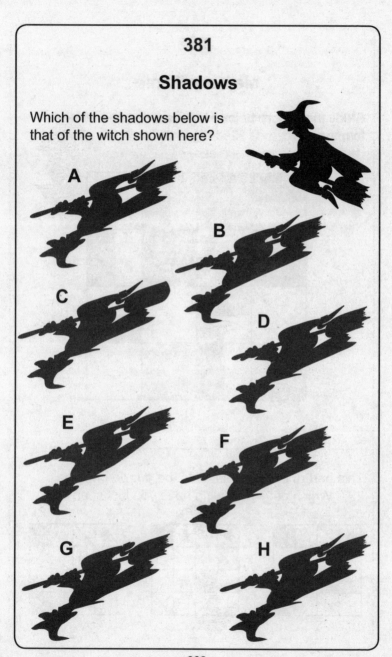

382

Jigsaw Puzzle

Which four shapes (two black and two white) can be fitted together to form the shape shown here?

The pieces may be rotated, but not flipped over.

 A

 B

C

 D

 E

 G

 F

 H

 I

 J

K

 L

 M

383

Buy-Buy

The Abstract Art Gallery has just sold a painting, after some deliberation by the customer, who took down each painting, turning it this way and that, before making a choice, and replacing five of the paintings haphazardly on the wall of the gallery.

Here are pictures of the display before and after the event. Which painting was purchased?

Before

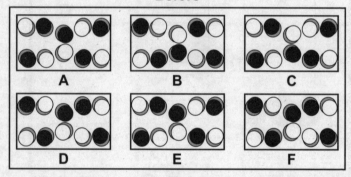

After

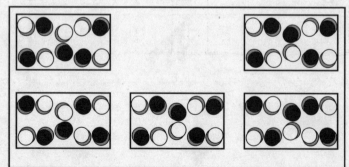

384

Sudoku

3	7			8	2		1	
		5	9				3	6
			6			7		
9	2				3		6	8
		4		2		1		
1	6		7				2	5
		3			8			
7	9				4	8		
	8		5	1			4	3

385

Word Ladder

Change one letter at a time (but not the position of any letter) to make a new word – and move from the word at the top of the ladder to the word at the bottom, using the exact number of rungs provided.

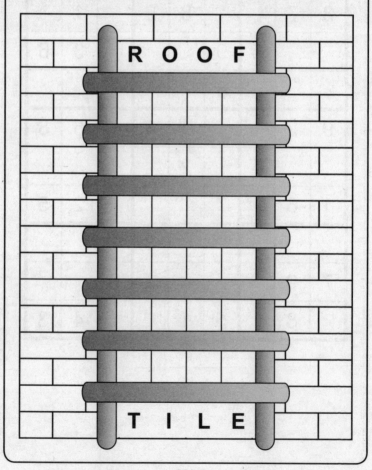

R O O F

T I L E

386

Treasure Hunt

The chart below gives directions to a hidden treasure behind the central black square in the grid.

Move the indicated number of spaces north, south, east, and west (e.g., 4N would mean four squares north) stopping at each square once only to arrive there.

At which square should you start?

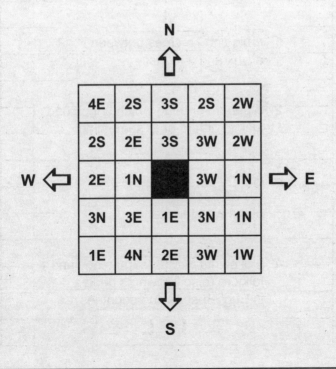

Wordpower

Which one of the four alternatives is the correct definition of the word shown below?

JYNX

1 A big cat – a cross between
a lynx and a jaguar

2 A person or thing which brings bad
luck to others or to something

3 A genus of bird, specifically
the wryneck, a relative
of the woodpecker

4 Evil spirits of Muslim theology and
folklore (also known as genies
in English-speaking countries)

388

Maze

Can you trace your way through this maze, without taking your pencil from the paper?

389

Wordwheel

How many words of three or more letters can you make from those in the wheel, without using plurals, abbreviations, or proper nouns in just three minutes?

The central letter must appear once in every word and no letter in a section of the wheel may be used more than once.

There is at least one nine-letter word in the wheel.

Nine-letter word(s):

Tile Twister

Place the eight tiles into the puzzle grid so that all adjacent numbers on each tile match up. Any tile may be rotated, but none may be flipped over.

3	3
1	1

2	2
1	4

3	2
2	1

3	4
2	3

1	2
1	2

1	4
1	3

1	3
3	2

3	3
2	4

				3	1
				2	1

391

Bermuda Triangle

Travel through the "Bermuda Triangle" by visiting one room at a time to collect a letter from each. You can enter the outside passageway as often as you like, but can only visit each room once.

When you've completed your tour, the 15 letters (in order) will spell out a word.

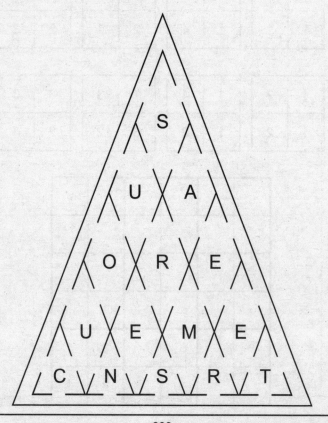

392

Shape Spotter

Which is the only shape to appear twice in the box below? You'll need a keen eye for this one, as some shapes overlap others!

393

Link Words

Fit different words into the central columns of the grid, so that each one links up with the words to either side, for example: table – lamp – shade.

When finished, read down the letters in the shaded squares to reveal another word, solving the clue below the grid.

READING					CASE
OVER					BACK
BEAN					POSITION
LANDS					CANAVERAL
ARCTIC					LIP
HUMAN					HORSE
GRIZZLY					HUG
CROSS					FALL

Clue: African desert

Word: _____

400

394

Half and Half

Pair off these groups of three letters to make eight types of building, each comprising six letters.

QUE   ACE   TLE   PLE

SCH   CHU   ODA   MUS

CAS   PAL   MOS   TEM

OOL   EUM   PAG   RCH

_____   _____

_____   _____

_____   _____

_____   _____

395

Couplets

The picture is of a central circle surrounded by shapes, linked to form six sets of three shapes apiece. Can you complete the puzzle by placing each of the two-letter groups below, one per shape, so that every set of three (the central circle, plus the two matching shapes diagonally opposite one another) forms a six-letter word? Whichever pair of letters you place in the central circle will appear in the middle of every word.

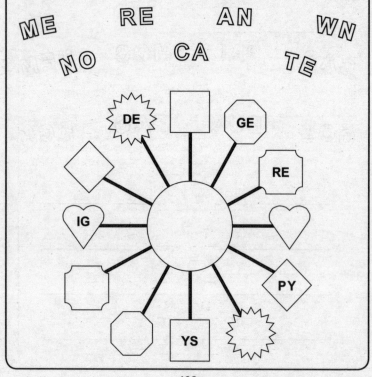

396

Keyword

On the face of it, this puzzle seems straightforward. Simply fill in the letters missing from words 1-8 and enter them into the numbered boxes, to reveal a hidden keyword.

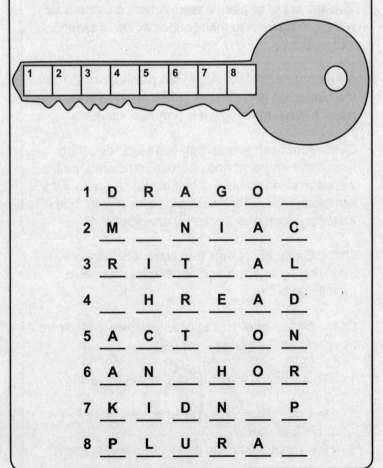

	1	2	3	4	5	6	7	8

1 D R A G O __

2 M __ N I A C

3 R I T __ A L

4 __ H R E A D

5 A C T __ O N

6 A N __ H O R

7 K I D N __ P

8 P L U R A __

Fractional Process

Eighteen airplanes were standing on the ground at Springfield Haven International Airport. Air traffic control had them listed as 1 to 18 inclusive.

Two-thirds of the planes were American, one-sixth were Canadian with the rest belonging to other nationalities.

Three-quarters of the American planes, two-thirds of the Canadian and all other nationalities planes were jets. Those remaining were propeller-driven.

Of the American planes that were jets, one-third were travelling east and of those remaining, half were travelling west, and half travelling south. Of the American planes that were propeller-driven, one was travelling east, one west, and one south.

Of the Canadian planes that were jets, all were travelling east. All other Canadian planes were travelling south.

Of the planes of other nationalities, two-thirds were travelling east and one-third west.

1. What was the total number of jets travelling west?
2. How many propeller-driven planes were travelling south?
3. How many American jets were travelling east?

Cut Out

Can you pair up shapes with the squares from which they were cut? Some may have been flipped over.

1

2

3

4

5

6

A

B

C

D

E

F

399

In at the Count

Precisely how many cars are in this picture?

400

Follow the Thread

These fishing lines have become tangled. Can you sort out which fish has been caught by each angler?

401

Colourful Wordsearch

```
E W O L L E Y N B E D
L N U C R R R P L I R
A L I X A U F E R N T
P N O R B C G W K E W
R Y D U A N C N J B G
I K A Z A M O V Y O O
C V C R V C A M C N L
O Y O I V P X U L Y D
T E V R I F R S Q A F
N M A N Y Z U B X A S
C K K J T E L R A C S
```

APRICOT   IVORY

AQUAMARINE   JET

AUBURN   ORANGE

AVOCADO   PINK

EBONY   SALMON

FERN   SCARLET

GOLD   YELLOW

402

Sequence Conundrum

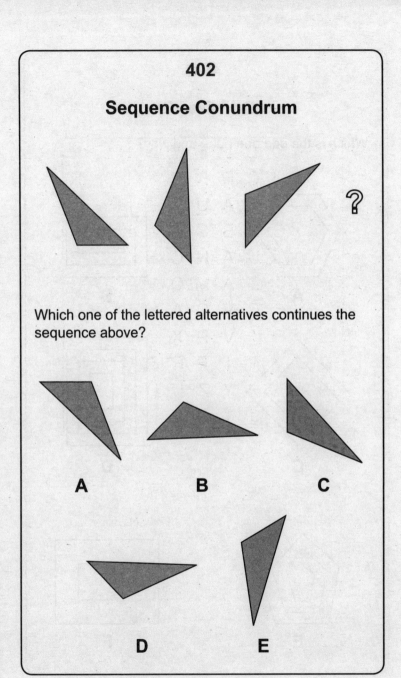

Which one of the lettered alternatives continues the sequence above?

A

B

C

D

E

403

Odd One Out

Which is the odd one out – and why?

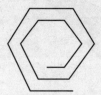

A

B

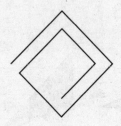

C

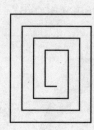

D

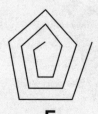

E

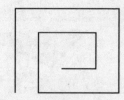

F

404

Sudoku

	1			3			4	
2		9	6		4	7		3
3			5		9			2
	9		2	5	3		6	
7		3				5		8
	6		9	7	8		3	
1			3		7			5
9		6	8		5	4		1
	5			9			2	

405

Wordfit

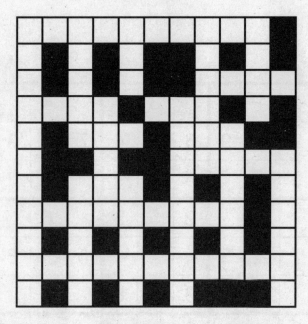

3 letters
APT
FEZ
LEG
LID
RAP

4 letters
NEON
PEEK
SOOT

5 letters
EXIST
FAULT
KEYED
NOVEL
ZEBRA

6 letters
PICKLE
SYNTAX
THIRTY

8 letters
PREPARED

9 letters
TRADEMARK

10 letters
SUNGLASSES

11 letters
ENLARGEMENT
STEPBROTHER

406

Spot the Difference

Which of these is different from the rest – and how?

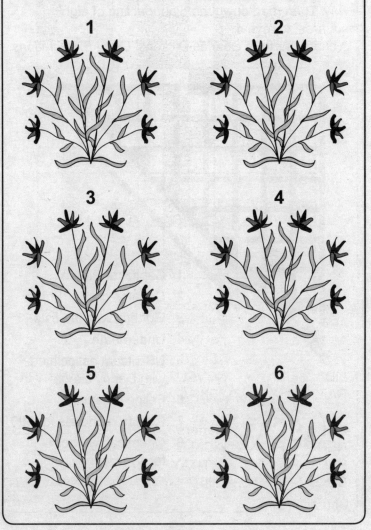

407

Character Assignation

Fill in the Across clues in this crossword in the normal way. Then read down the diagonal line of eight squares, to reveal:
A character from Charles Dickens' *Great Expectations*.

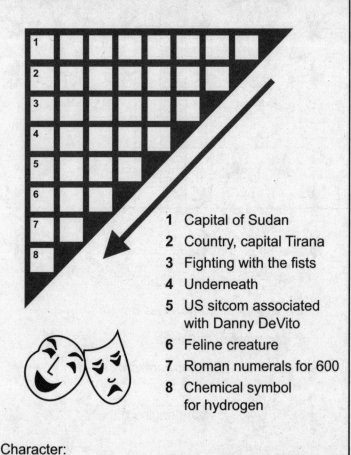

1 Capital of Sudan
2 Country, capital Tirana
3 Fighting with the fists
4 Underneath
5 US sitcom associated with Danny DeVito
6 Feline creature
7 Roman numerals for 600
8 Chemical symbol for hydrogen

Character: ___ ___ ___ ___ ___ ___ ___ ___

408

Pyracross

Solve the clues on each level of the pyramid and reveal the word in the central column of bricks, a clue for which is: South American river.

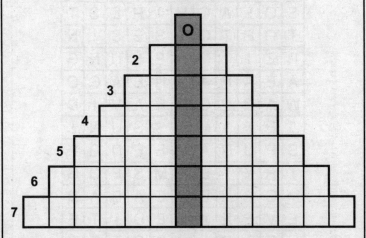

2 Boat built by Noah

3 River which flows through Paris

4 Country also known as Burma

5 Largest city in Alaska

6 Body of water surrounding the North Pole (6,5)

7 One skilled in the ringing of bells

HIDDEN WORD: _____

Do It Yourself!

The listed words all appear in this crossword – you just need to blank out the unwanted squares…

S	O	F	A	C	H	A	R	E	S	T
T	O	R	T	O	I	S	E	S	I	N
R	Z	I	I	M	P	F	L	U	N	G
A	E	A	P	A	C	R	E	A	G	O
W	A	R	P	O	R	E	A	V	I	D
A	P	E	A	M	A	S	S	U	N	I
S	P	U	R	A	V	E	E	D	G	E
T	R	Y	T	E	E	M	S	E	G	G
M	O	A	N	E	D	E	A	B	A	R
E	V	E	E	X	P	E	D	I	T	E
H	E	I	R	I	S	K	S	T	E	T

ACRE	EGRET	RELEASE
AMASS	EXPEDITE	REST
APPROVE	FRIAR	SINGING
AVID	HEIR	SPUR
COMA	LUNG	STRAW
CRAVE	MEEK	TEEM
DEBIT	MOAN	TORTOISE
EDGE	PARTNER	WARP

410

Letters Crossword

Each clue consists of letters in alphabetical order.
Rearrange these to form words, then fill the grid.

Across

2 AINOORT (7)
7 AEGNR (5)
8 ACLLO (5)
10 EERW (4)
11 AERR (4)
12 ADEL (4)
14 EOSW (4)
16 ANORS (5)
18 DEPRU (5)
19 AEKRSST (7)

Down

1 AACDELNRS (9)
2 EGLO (4)
3 DEEORRR (7)
4 ACR (3)
5 EILS (4)
6 DEHINORSU (9)
9 AKORRTW (7)
13 AILR (4)
15 NOSU (4)
17 APS (3)

411

Around the Clock

Travel around the clock, one hour at a time, making twelve words all ending with the central letter. The letters to be placed in the empty squares are to be found in the segment clockwise of the number to be filled. We've completed one already, in order to get you off to a timely start…

Now take the central letter of every even-numbered word and rearrange these to form another, meaning: Major South American river.

___ ____ ___ ___ ____ ___

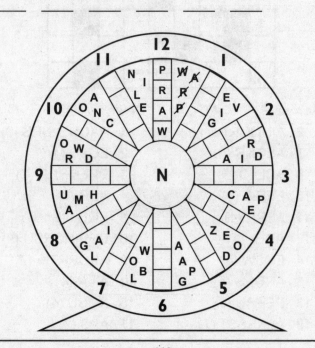

412

Around the Block

You won't need a starting block to get you under way, because it isn't a race! Just arrange the six-letter solutions to the clues into the six blocks around each clue number.

Write the answers in a clockwise or anticlockwise direction and you'll find that the last answer fits into the first; the main problem will be to decide in which square to put the first letter of each word...

1 Capital of Saudi Arabia
2 Strong need to drink
3 Heaviness
4 Sign of the zodiac after Taurus
5 Threat, peril
6 State capital of New York

413

Roundword

Write the answer to each clue into the grid, working in a clockwise direction.

Every solution overlaps the next by either one, two, or three letters and each solution starts in its numbered section.

The solution to the final clue ends with the letter in the first square.

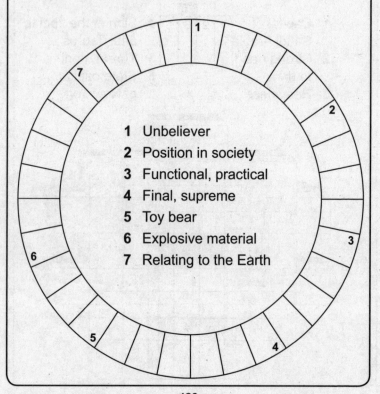

1 Unbeliever
2 Position in society
3 Functional, practical
4 Final, supreme
5 Toy bear
6 Explosive material
7 Relating to the Earth

414

Square Filler

The clues list the groups of adjacent blacked-out squares for each row and column, as you can see in this example:

Any adjacent blacked-out squares must have at least one white square between them and the next set of adjacent blacked-out squares.

Just follow the clues to fill in each row and column.

415

Dice Section

Printed onto every one of the six numbered dice are six letters (one per side), which can be rearranged to form the answer to each clue; however, some sides are invisible to you. Use the clues and write every answer into the grid. When correctly filled, the letters in the shaded squares, reading in the order 1 to 6, will spell out a city in southern Texas.

1 Wooden-headed hammer

2 40th President of the USA

3 Tusked marine mammal

4 Verse

5 Second book of the Old Testament

6 Of inferior workmanship and materials

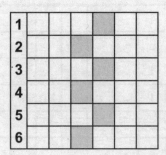

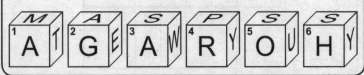

416

Pyramid Plus

Every brick in this pyramid contains a number which is the sum of the two numbers below it, so that F = A + B, etc.

Just work out the missing numbers!

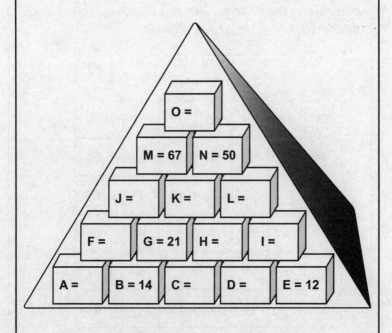

417

Total Concentration

The blank squares below should be filled with whole numbers between 1 and 20 inclusive, any of which may occur more than once, or not at all.

The numbers in every horizontal row add up to the totals on the right, as do the two long diagonal lines; whilst those in every vertical column add up to the totals along the bottom. Can you discover the missing numbers?

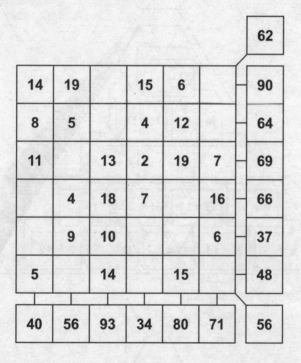

						62
14	19		15	6		90
8	5		4	12		64
11		13	2	19	7	69
	4	18	7		16	66
	9	10			6	37
5		14		15		48
40	56	93	34	80	71	56

418

Hexagony

Can you place the hexagons into the grid, so that where any hexagon touches another along a straight line, the contents of both triangles are the same? No rotation of any hexagon is allowed!

419

Number Fit

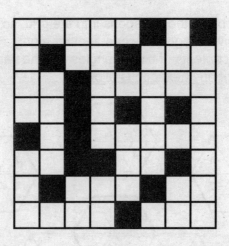

2 digits	3 digits	5 digits
28	312	15259
35	333	23921
59	395	32190
63	411	49218
66	594	54422
73	775	
74		
78	**4 digits**	**7 digits**
84	1537	2851263
90	4848	
	5319	

420

Sudoku

4			7					
	3			6	9		2	1
	9	6		5		4	3	
6	2	4	8			1		
		5				7		
		1			4	9	6	8
	6	8		7		3	1	
7	5		1	4			8	
					2			9

421

Box Clever

When the box below is folded to form a cube, just one of the five options (A, B, C, D, or E) can be produced. Which?

422

Sequence Conundrum

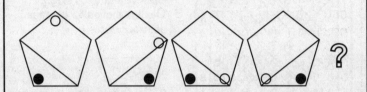

Which one of the lettered alternatives continues the
sequence above?

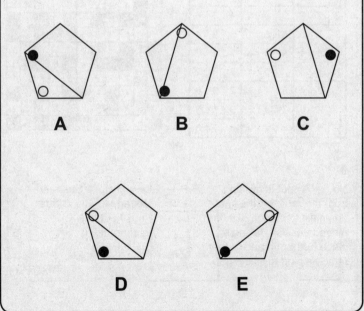

Solutions

1

2

D – The black circle moves an extra 45 degrees clockwise at each stage. The line moves 45 degrees anticlockwise.

3

B – In all the others the circle and square overlap. In B the triangle and square overlap.

4

4	5	9	1	7	3	6	2	8
6	1	2	8	5	4	7	3	9
8	7	3	2	9	6	1	5	4
7	3	5	4	6	2	8	9	1
2	6	1	9	8	5	3	4	7
9	4	8	7	3	1	5	6	2
3	9	4	5	1	7	2	8	6
1	2	6	3	4	8	9	7	5
5	8	7	6	2	9	4	1	3

5

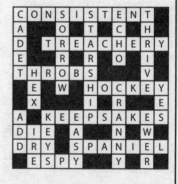

6

No 5 – A spot is missing from the roof and the spot originally to the left of it has moved position, taking a place further up and further right, helping to fill the gap.

7

1 Lava lamp, 2 Strange, 3 Mozart, 4 Aisle, 5 Soar, 6 Pup, 7 PA, 8 N.
The character is: PETER PAN

Solutions

8

2 Hen, 3 Minsk, 4 Algeria,
5 Patagonia, 6 Minneapolis,
7 Ventriloquist.
The word is:
SENEGAL

9

10

11

1 Drill, 2 Expel, 3 Anvil,
4 Dwell, 5 Yodel, 6 Basic,
7 Peril, 8 Trawl, 9 Mural,
10 Vital, 11 Growl, 12 Focal.
The word is:
ASPECT

12

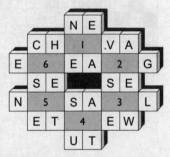

13

1 Library, 2 Yellow, 3 Lower,
4 Ruminated, 5 Tedious,
6 Usurer, 7 Rill.

14

15

1 Pampas, 2 Closet,
3 Stupid, 4 Icebox,
5 Obeyed, 6 Vienna.
The cartoon character is:
POPEYE

Solutions

16

A = 7, B = 13, C = 12,
D = 6, E = 2, F = 20, G = 25,
H = 18, I = 8, J = 45, K = 43,
L = 26, M = 88, N = 69,
O = 157.

18

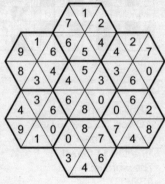

17

							75
10	1	17	14	6	20		68
2	2	11	11	15	20		61
10	9	1	19	16	13		68
12	18	3	19	3	16		71
5	13	12	15	17	7		69
5	4	18	4	8	14		53
44	47	62	82	65	90		63

19

6	3	8	3	8	■	5	5
2			7	1		9	1
5		1	6	6	4	7	8
8		9	9			0	■
■	7		1	5	9	0	2
2	3	2		2	0		6
■	2	9	5	4		6	■
5	0	■	4	2	7	7	8

21

D

22

B – At each stage the ellipse moves 45 degrees clockwise and the white dot moves 90 degrees anticlockwise within the ellipse.

20

1	5	6	7	2	4	3	9	8
3	2	9	8	6	5	4	7	1
7	4	8	1	9	3	2	5	6
4	9	7	5	3	8	6	1	2
8	6	5	9	1	2	7	3	4
2	1	3	4	7	6	9	8	5
5	3	1	6	4	9	8	2	7
6	7	2	3	8	1	5	4	9
9	8	4	2	5	7	1	6	3

Solutions

23

1 Clever, 2 Fabric, 3 Glance,
4 Norway, 5 Sahara, 6 Warsaw.

24

$7 \times 8 - 5 + 6 = 57$

25

♎	☐	■	⌘	◆
⌘	■	◆	☐	♎
☐	⌘	♎	◆	■
◆	♎	☐	■	⌘
■	◆	⌘	♎	☐

26

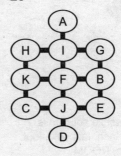

27

28

1 D, 2 A, 3 C, 4 E, 5 B.

29

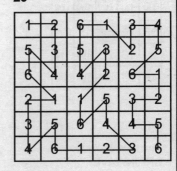

30

Please refer back to the
original puzzle and check
your answer against that.

31

E

Solutions

32

B

M

D

K

33

C

34

3	2	4	9	1	5	6	8	7
7	1	5	8	6	2	4	9	3
8	9	6	7	3	4	1	2	5
4	3	2	6	8	1	5	7	9
6	7	1	3	5	9	2	4	8
5	8	9	2	4	7	3	1	6
1	5	3	4	9	8	7	6	2
2	6	8	1	7	3	9	5	4
9	4	7	5	2	6	8	3	1

35

One possible solution is:
WASH, lash, last, lost, loot, loom, ROOM

36

2S	3S	4S	1E	2W
1N	1N	1W	3W	1W
3E	1E		1S	3W
2E	1S	2E	3W	1N
4E	2E	3N	3W	3N

37

The correct definition is 1.

38

39

The nine-letter word is:
BRAINWAVE

Solutions

40

1	1	1	1	1	3
3	2	2	3	3	1
3	2	2	3	3	1
3	3	3	4	4	2
3	3	3	4	4	2
4	1	1	2	2	3

41

The word is:
CONSERVATIONIST

42

43

1 Dust, 2 News, 3 Rock,
4 Farm, 5 Cake, 6 Pass or
Pine, 7 Iron, 8 Down.
The word is: TERRAPIN

44

The currency units are:
DOLLAR, ESCUDO, FORINT,
GULDEN, MARKKA,
PESETA, ROUBLE, SHEKEL.

45

The words are: BECKON,
FICKLE, HOCKEY, JACKAL,
POCKET, SICKLY.

46

1 Chosen, 2 Eighty, 3 Prince,
4 Dancer, 5 Nearly, 6 Blouse,
7 Zealot, 8 Embers.
The word is: HEIRLOOM

47

9 – 2 teenagers, 4 men, and
3 women.

48

1 F, 2 A, 3 E, 4 C, 5 D, 6 B.

49

45

50

1–C, 2–A, 3–E, 4–B, 5–D.

Solutions

51

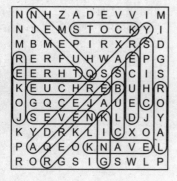

52

A – Each figure then has a mirror image.

53

C – A is the same as E with black/white circle reversal. Similarly B is the same as D and F is the same as G.

54

4	7	9	3	1	2	8	5	6
6	1	5	9	7	8	4	2	3
3	8	2	4	6	5	9	1	7
8	4	6	1	2	3	7	9	5
5	9	7	6	8	4	1	3	2
2	3	1	5	9	7	6	4	8
7	6	4	2	5	9	3	8	1
1	5	3	8	4	6	2	7	9
9	2	8	7	3	1	5	6	4

55

56

1 – The pen has changed position in relation to the book.

57

1 Nightcap, 2 Fanfare,
3 Ablaze or Aflame,
4 Wager, 5 Twig, 6 Sty, 7 In,
8 T.
The character is:
PEER GYNT

Solutions

58

2 Boa, 3 Atlas, 4 Namibia,
5 Pistachio, 6 Sagittarius,
7 Massachusetts.
The word is:
GOLIATH

60

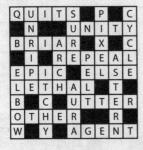

62

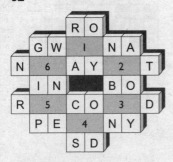

64

59

61

1 Braid or Rabid, 2 Dryad,
3 Yield, 4 Caged, 5 Build,
6 Freed, 7 Paled or Plead,
8 Lurid, 9 Nomad, 10 Blend,
11 Rapid, 12 Zoned.
The word is:
ENERGY

63

1 Estuary, 2 Yeast, 3 Stereo,
4 Omega, 5 Garlic, 6 Iceland,
7 Delete.

65

1 Double, 2 Shared, 3 Nectar,
4 Admire, 5 Karate, 6 Kansas.
The comic-book superhero is:
BATMAN

Solutions

66

A = 3, B = 11, C = 15, D = 8,
E = 16, F = 14, G = 26,
H = 23, I = 24, J = 40,
K = 49, L = 47, M = 89,
N = 96, O = 185.

67

						44
1	14	2	4	12	17	50
8	9	18	10	4	7	56
15	15	10	7	2	12	61
5	11	5	14	13	13	61
16	3	11	20	16	6	72
8	19	3	6	1	9	46
53	71	49	71	48	64	59

68

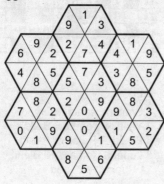

69

2	3	4	5	0	■	1	2
2	■	4	1	■	3	7	0
5	8	■	3	7	8	2	0
7	2	5	5	4	■	3	0
■	4	■	6	0	4	5	1
6	8	4	■	3	■	■	1
8	■	7	8	4	8	2	■
5	2	3	■	■	8	2	3

70

5	8	4	9	3	1	2	6	7
3	7	6	2	8	4	1	5	9
1	9	2	7	5	6	3	4	8
7	2	9	4	6	3	5	8	1
8	4	3	1	9	5	7	2	6
6	1	5	8	2	7	9	3	4
9	5	7	3	4	8	6	1	2
2	3	8	6	1	9	4	7	5
4	6	1	5	7	2	8	9	3

71

D

72

C – Just the left half of the
three figures is being repeated.

438

Solutions

73

1 Bisect, 2 Dozing, 3 Knight,
4 Osprey, 5 Sprint, 6 Wonder.

74

$28 + 8 - 2 \times 3 = 102$

75

■	◆	☐	♎	⌘
⌘	■	♎	☐	◆
☐	⌘	◆	■	♎
♎	☐	⌘	◆	■
◆	♎	■	⌘	☐

76

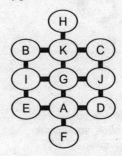

77

78

1 E, 2 D, 3 C, 4 A, 5 B.

79

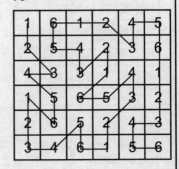

80

Please refer back to the
original puzzle and check
your answer against that.

81

C

Solutions

82

83

A

84

2	5	8	6	3	7	4	9	1
4	3	6	5	9	1	7	8	2
1	9	7	2	4	8	5	6	3
6	7	2	4	8	3	1	5	9
8	4	9	7	1	5	2	3	6
3	1	5	9	6	2	8	4	7
5	8	3	1	7	6	9	2	4
7	6	4	8	2	9	3	1	5
9	2	1	3	5	4	6	7	8

85

One possible solution is:
DUCK, suck, sock, soak,
    soap, swap, SWAN

86

4E	2E	4S	4S	2W
1N	2E	2E	1S	4W
2E	1N		3W	1S
2E	1N	2N	3W	1W
4E	1N	1W	3W	2N

87

The correct definition is 4.

88

89

The nine-letter word is:
THICKENED

Solutions

90

1	1	1	3	3	4
4	2	2	2	2	4
4	2	2	2	2	4
1	4	4	3	3	2
1	4	4	3	3	2
2	1	1	4	4	1

91

The word is:
PHARMACEUTICALS

92

93

1 Ward, 2 Blue, 3 Gold,
4 Pole, 5 Call, 6 Star,
7 Wise, 8 Wood.
The word is: RELEASED

94

The herbs and spices are:
BORAGE, CHIVES, ENDIVE,
FENNEL, GINGER, HYSSOP,
LOVAGE, NUTMEG.

95

The words are: COBALT,
DEBATE, EMBALM,
RIBALD, TOBAGO,
URBANE.

96

1 Abroad, 2 Pauper, 3 Resort,
4 Aiming, 5 Muster, 6 Avenue,
7 Desert, 8 Python.
The word is: BURGUNDY

97

11

98

1 A, 2 E, 3 D, 4 F, 5 B, 6 C.

99

64

100

1–E, 2–B, 3–D, 4–C, 5–A.

Solutions

101

102

D – The black dot moves two corners anticlockwise at each stage and the triangle moves two sides clockwise at each stage.

103

A – The others are all the same figure rotated. A is a reflection of the other figures, not a rotation.

104

8	3	7	5	4	6	9	1	2
1	9	4	2	7	8	5	3	6
2	5	6	9	3	1	7	4	8
5	1	3	6	2	9	8	7	4
6	4	8	3	1	7	2	9	5
9	7	2	8	5	4	3	6	1
3	6	9	1	8	2	4	5	7
7	8	5	4	6	3	1	2	9
4	2	1	7	9	5	6	8	3

105

106

2 – Two of the bands (near to the head of the rocket) have swapped colour.

107

1 Backlash, 2 Tripoli, 3 Vicuña or Alpaca, 4 Sinew, 5 Asia, 6 TNT, 7 pH, 8 A. The character is: HIAWATHA

Solutions

108

2 Sly, 3 Egypt, 4 Slumber,
5 Semaphore, 6 Albuquerque,
7 Procrastinate.
The word is:
OLYMPUS

110

112

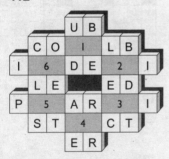

114

109

111

1 Owner, 2 Floor, 3 Paper,
4 Truer, 5 Whirr, 6 Error,
7 River, 8 Juror, 9 Donor,
10 Incur, 11 Flair, 12 Laser.
The word is:
CURSOR

113

1 Tabasco, 2 Coaxed,
3 Edict, 4 Titian, 5 Anxiety,
6 Tycoon, 7 Nudist.

115

1 Apache, 2 Zealot,
3 Hebrew, 4 Target, 5 Dozing,
6 Ghetto.
The book by Stephen King is:
CARRIE

Solutions

116

A = 9, B = 22, C = 5, D = 6,
E = 4, F = 31, G = 27,
H = 11, I = 10, J = 58,
K = 38, L = 21, M = 96,
N = 59, O = 155.

118

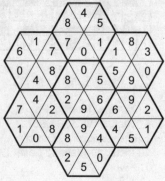

117

							58
17	11	7	3	19	9	66	
4	14	1	6	12	3	40	
6	13	10	18	18	7	72	
20	17	13	2	8	11	71	
5	2	9	1	15	19	51	
4	16	12	20	10	8	70	
56	73	52	50	82	57	66	

119

9	7	6	■	3	7	6	■
8	■	3	4	■	9	3	7
■	2	5	■	8	0	■	8
1	0	7	4	■	■	1	6
6	4	■	8	■	■	2	3
5	■	■	9	2	3	5	0
0	■	5	■	8	0	3	■
9	9	3	0	4	6	7	■

121

C

122

E – The black square which starts at the bottom is moving one row up at each stage. The black square which starts at the top right is moving one column left at each stage.

120

5	6	9	7	8	3	1	4	2
1	8	7	5	2	4	3	9	6
3	4	2	1	9	6	7	5	8
4	9	1	2	6	5	8	7	3
7	3	5	4	1	8	6	2	9
6	2	8	9	3	7	4	1	5
2	7	3	6	4	9	5	8	1
9	5	6	8	7	1	2	3	4
8	1	4	3	5	2	9	6	7

Solutions

123

1 Apiary, 2 Fiasco, 3 Mutual, 4 Recent, 5 Utopia, 6 Yogurt.

124

16 – 4 + 5 x 2 = 34

125

■	⌘	♎	□	◆
□	♎	⌘	◆	■
◆	■	□	⌘	♎
⌘	◆	■	♎	□
♎	□	◆	■	⌘

126

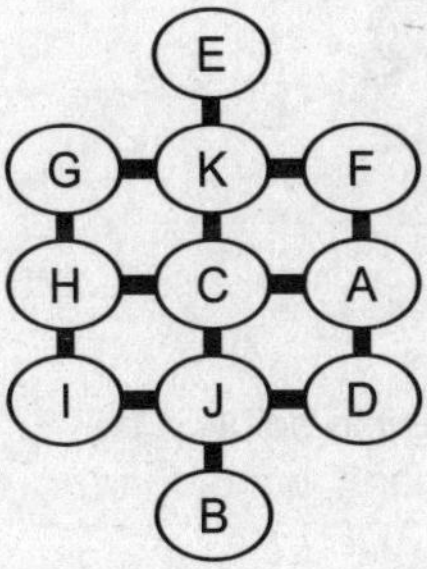

127

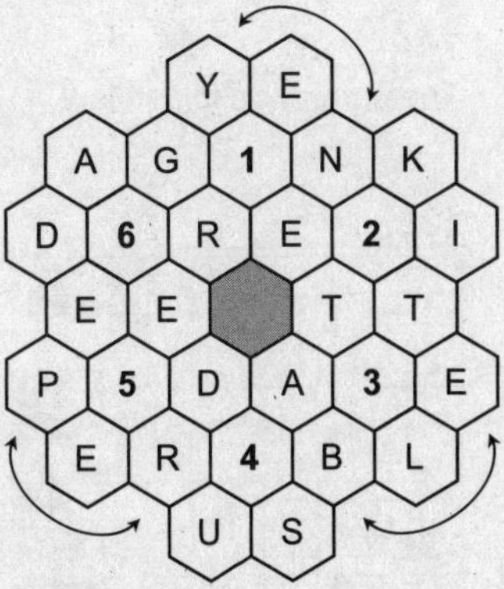

128

1 E, 2 B, 3 D, 4 C, 5 A.

129

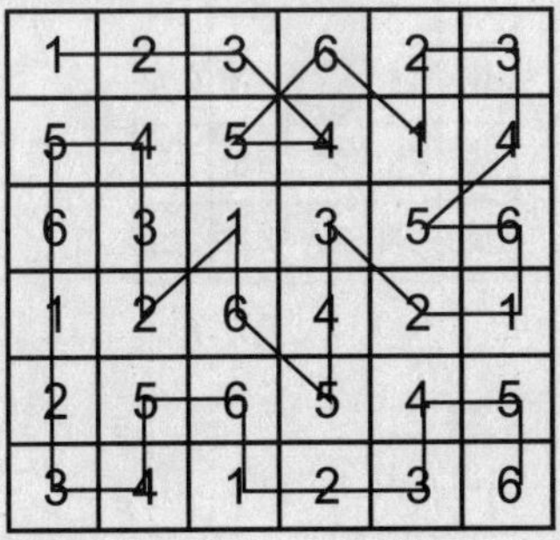

130

Please refer back to the original puzzle and check your answer against that.

131

A

Solutions

132

J   F

E   B

133
D

134

6	4	8	9	3	2	5	7	1
9	3	5	6	1	7	2	8	4
1	7	2	5	8	4	9	3	6
7	2	1	3	9	8	6	4	5
3	8	6	1	4	5	7	2	9
4	5	9	2	7	6	8	1	3
5	6	7	4	2	3	1	9	8
8	1	4	7	5	9	3	6	2
2	9	3	8	6	1	4	5	7

135

One possible solution is:
HAND, band, bond, fond,
font, FOOT

136

3S	1E	4S	2W	4W
1S	2E	2S	3S	1N
4E	2S		2W	2W
3E	2N	2E	1N	1S
3N	1N	2W	4N	3N

137

The correct definition is 2.

138

139

The nine-letter word is:
FABRICATE

Solutions

140

2	2	2	1	1	2
1	1	1	4	4	3
1	1	1	4	4	3
4	2	2	3	3	1
4	2	2	3	3	1
3	4	4	3	3	4

141

The word is:
CO-OPERATIVENESS

142

143

1 Band, 2 Part, 3 Cold,
4 Lock, 5 Ring, 6 Chop,
7 Food, 8 Worm.
The word is: BALLROOM

144

The nautical terms are:
ANCHOR, ASTERN, CRUISE,
FATHOM, JETSAM, MARINA,
SAILOR, TILLER.

145

The words are: ANORAK,
CHORUS, FLORAL, POORLY,
SCORCH, THORAX.

146

1 Reject, 2 Sinful, 3 Absurd,
4 Ending, 5 Travel, 6 Avenge,
7 Notice, 8 Obtain.
The word is: JUBILANT

147

19

148

1 B, 2 A, 3 F, 4 D, 5 C, 6 E.

149

72

150

1–D, 2–A, 3–B, 4–E, 5–C.

Solutions

151

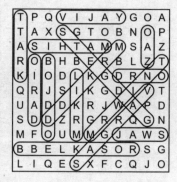

152

B – The figures alternate three sides/four sides and the number of dots alternates one/two.

153

D – In all the others the segments are in the same order reading clockwise or anticlockwise. In D two of the segments have been swapped round.

154

9	7	8	3	1	6	4	2	5
2	1	4	5	7	9	6	3	8
3	5	6	2	4	8	7	1	9
1	6	3	7	9	2	5	8	4
7	9	2	8	5	4	3	6	1
4	8	5	6	3	1	2	9	7
8	4	7	9	2	3	1	5	6
6	2	1	4	8	5	9	7	3
5	3	9	1	6	7	8	4	2

155

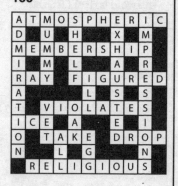

156

4 – The shorter flower has an extra petal near to the stalk.

157

1 Treasury, 2 Picasso, 3 Viking, 4 Corgi, 5 Crab, 6 Ewe, 7 Ta, 8 R.
The character is:
YOGI BEAR

Solutions

158

2 Bet, 3 Alamo, 4 Austria,
5 Armstrong, 6 Buffalo Bill,
7 Liechtenstein.
The word is:
SEATTLE

159

M	A	G	M	A		B		T		B
	M			B	R	A	V	A	D	O
B	U	G	L	E		B		X		X
	S			D	A	Y	T	I	M	E
B	E	N	T		B		E			R
	D		R	O	O	T	S		D	
B			O		V		T	R	E	E
A	N	O	T	H	E	R			M	
N		A		E		A	S	P	I	C
A	R	T	L	E	S	S			S	
L		H		L		P	A	N	E	L

160

L	A	W	N		S	I	F	T
O			A	S	K			U
P	O	R	P	O	I	S	E	S
E	R	A		M		P		K
	B	L	E	E	P	E	R	
A		L		D		C	U	T
J	A	Y	W	A	L	K	E	R
A			E	Y	E			A
R	A	F	T		D	U	T	Y

161

1 Inept, 2 Midst, 3 Pilot,
4 Tenet, 5 Wheat, 6 Roast,
7 Heart, 8 Sprat, 9 Giant,
10 Asset, 11 Ascot or Coast,
12 Motet.
The word is:
STRAND

162

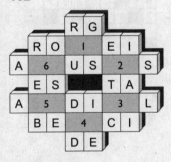

163

1 Galaxy, 2 Xylophone,
3 Neptune, 4 Neglect,
5 Trap, 6 Rapier, 7 Erring.

164

165

1 Helper, 2 Writer, 3 Kirsch,
4 Potent, 5 Absorb, 6 Gallon.
The weapon is:
PISTOL

Solutions

166

A = 3, B = 1, C = 20, D = 5,
E = 18, F = 4, G = 21,
H = 25, I = 23, J = 25,
K = 46, L = 48, M = 71,
N = 94, O = 165.

167

						68
14	11	5	4	19	17	70
5	9	15	10	16	4	59
12	6	20	18	9	8	73
18	19	8	1	16	14	76
6	2	15	1	13	2	39
7	20	17	7	3	3	57
62	67	80	41	76	48	60

168

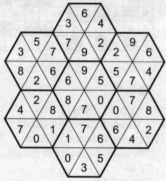

169

8	3	6	4		1	8	
9	7		5	2	2	0	0
3	3	5	0	0	6	7	
6	0		2	9	4	7	7
2		1	2	7		6	
2	4	3			3	3	4
	4	0	8	2	3		0
1	6	7	8	8		5	1

170

4	5	9	7	8	1	2	3	6
1	2	3	4	5	6	8	9	7
6	8	7	3	2	9	1	4	5
7	1	8	5	6	3	9	2	4
9	3	6	2	4	8	7	5	1
2	4	5	9	1	7	3	6	8
5	9	4	1	7	2	6	8	3
8	7	2	6	3	4	5	1	9
3	6	1	8	9	5	4	7	2

171

A

172

A – At each stage the white dot is moving top to bottom and the black dot is moving right to left. The line moves 45 degrees anticlockwise at each stage.

450

Solutions

173
1 Exhale, 2 Holier, 3 Junket,
4 Object, 5 Thesis, 6 Uranus.

174
$37 - 17 \times 3 + 19 = 79$

175

□	■	⌘	♎	◆
■	◆	□	⌘	♎
◆	⌘	♎	□	■
⌘	♎	◆	■	□
♎	□	■	◆	⌘

176

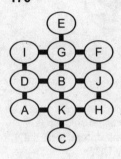

177

178
1 B, 2 E, 3 C, 4 D, 5 A.

179

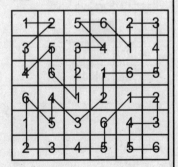

180
Please refer back to the
original puzzle and check
your answer against that.

181
G

Solutions

182

G   D

A   H

183

F

184

9	6	7	1	3	5	8	2	4
2	5	8	7	4	6	9	3	1
4	3	1	9	2	8	5	6	7
5	9	3	6	7	4	2	1	8
8	1	2	5	9	3	4	7	6
6	7	4	2	8	1	3	9	5
1	4	6	3	5	9	7	8	2
7	8	9	4	6	2	1	5	3
3	2	5	8	1	7	6	4	9

185

One possible solution is:
NEAP, neat, teat, tent, tint,
tine, TIDE

186

2E	4S	1S	1E	3W
3S	1W	2E	2S	1W
3E	1S		2S	3W
1N	2N	2W	1E	2W
2E	3E	2N	4N	2N

187

The correct definition is 3.

188

189

The nine-letter word is:
HAILSTONE

Solutions

190

2	1	1	4	4	3
3	3	3	2	2	4
3	3	3	2	2	4
2	2	2	1	1	3
2	2	2	1	1	3
4	4	4	3	3	4

191

The word is:
AERODYNAMICALLY

192

193

1 Reef, 2 Bare, 3 Ship,
4 Stop, 5 Wash, 6 Fish,
7 Suit, 8 Fall or Hold.
The word is: FAITHFUL

194

The drinks are: BRANDY,
CLARET, COFFEE,
COGNAC, GRAPPA,
KIRSCH, SHERRY, WHISKY.

195

The words are: BEDAUB,
JUDAIC, MADAME,
ORDAIN, PEDALO,
UPDATE.

196

1 Allude, 2 Prefix, 3 Lesson,
4 Urgent, 5 Odious, 6 Killer,
7 Abound, 8 Wander.
The word is: DELUSION

197

3

198

1 E, 2 B, 3 C, 4 A, 5 F, 6 D.

199

78

200

1–B, 2–C, 3–A, 4–D, 5–E.

Solutions

201

202

C – Looking across, in each square the top left quarter alternates white dot/black dot. In the top right quarter the line moves 45 degrees clockwise. In the bottom left the line moves 90 degrees clockwise. In the bottom right the line moves 45 degrees clockwise.

203

B – In the others an upturned mouth has the curl pointing left and a downturned mouth has the curl pointing right. B has a downturned mouth with the curl pointing left.

204

1	9	3	8	4	2	7	5	6
6	2	5	7	1	3	8	9	4
4	7	8	9	6	5	2	3	1
2	1	4	5	3	7	6	8	9
8	3	7	6	2	9	1	4	5
5	6	9	1	8	4	3	7	2
9	8	1	3	5	6	4	2	7
3	5	2	4	7	1	9	6	8
7	4	6	2	9	8	5	1	3

205

206

6 – Three of the bricks have been replaced by one, bottom right.

207

1 Damascus, 2 Anagram, 3 Bonsai, 4 Night, 5 Bath, 6 She, 7 Or, 8 S.
The character is:
SMITHERS

Solutions

208

2 Bed, 3 Dumbo, 4 Tripoli,
5 Beethoven, 6 Near-sighted,
7 Jefferson City.
The word is:
MEMPHIS

210

212

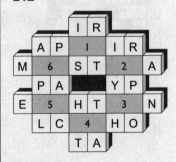

214

209

211

1 Tense, 2 Snake, 3 Juice,
4 Ample or Maple, 5 House,
6 Piece, 7 Choke, 8 Waste,
9 Halve, 10 Solve, 11 Swore
or Worse, 12 Theme.
The word is:
ELAPSE

213

1 Kilogram, 2 Ramadan,
3 Danube, 4 Beware,
5 Reverse, 6 Severe,
7 Embark.

215

1 Revoke, 2 Extend,
3 Wasted, 4 Leader,
5 Drowsy, 6 Dragon.
The Canadian city is:
OTTAWA

Solutions

216

A = 8, B = 5, C = 9, D = 3,
E = 12, F = 13, G = 14,
H = 12, I = 15, J = 27,
K = 26, L = 27, M = 53,
N = 53, O = 106.

218

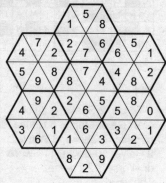

217

						65
10	20	7	19	14	6	76
8	1	2	11	15	20	57
1	17	2	10	11	16	57
16	3	18	12	5	17	71
9	13	4	4	15	12	57
3	14	13	19	5	18	72
47	68	46	75	65	89	58

219

	7	6	7	9		5	9
3	2	1				7	1
3		2	2	4	3		
9	2	3		8	6	7	
4	4		2	4		3	9
7	2	1		5	8	3	4
	3	6	0	0	4	1	
6	6	5			9	0	2

221

B

222

B – At each stage the large hexagon is being constructed one side at a time clockwise. The small hexagon is being dismantled one side at a time anticlockwise.

220

5	6	8	7	1	2	9	4	3
9	4	7	3	5	6	1	8	2
1	2	3	9	8	4	5	6	7
8	5	1	2	7	3	4	9	6
4	7	6	8	9	1	3	2	5
3	9	2	4	6	5	7	1	8
2	1	9	5	3	8	6	7	4
7	8	5	6	4	9	2	3	1
6	3	4	1	2	7	8	5	9

Solutions

223

1 Grotto, 2 Impede, 3 Liquor,
4 Nebula, 5 Sloppy, 6 Vishnu.

224

$52 + 4 \times 2 - 18 = 94$

225

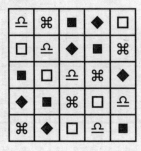

226

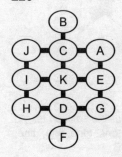

227

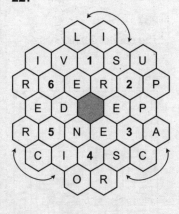

228

1 B, 2 E, 3 C, 4 D, 5 A.

229

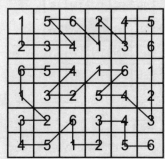

230

Please refer back to the
original puzzle and check
your answer against that.

231

E

Solutions

232

M

I

D

A

235

One possible solution is:
TOSS, tons, tone, tine, dine,
     DICE

236

1S	4S	2W	3S	3W
3S	1E	1N	1N	1S
1S	1S		3W	3W
4E	2N	1N	1W	3N
2E	3E	1E	3N	3N

239

The nine-letter word is:
IDENTICAL

233

B

234

5	4	2	8	7	9	3	6	1
9	8	6	1	3	5	2	4	7
7	3	1	6	2	4	9	5	8
4	5	7	2	1	6	8	9	3
6	2	8	3	9	7	5	1	4
3	1	9	5	4	8	6	7	2
1	6	5	4	8	2	7	3	9
2	9	4	7	6	3	1	8	5
8	7	3	9	5	1	4	2	6

237

The correct definition is 4.

238

Solutions

240

2	4	4	2	2	4
4	1	1	3	3	3
4	1	1	3	3	3
3	2	2	2	2	1
3	2	2	2	2	1
1	1	1	4	4	4

241

The word is:
INSTRUMENTALIST

242

243

1 Hood, 2 Chin, 3 Vine,
4 Slip, 5 Road, 6 Bill,
7 Town, 8 Good.
The word is: DIVIDING

244

The countries are: BELIZE,
CANADA, FRANCE,
GREECE, ISRAEL, JORDAN,
TAIWAN, ZAMBIA.

245

The words are: ACIDIC,
BRIDAL, BRIDGE, FRIDAY,
MAIDEN, SPIDER.

246

1 Hornet, 2 Expert, 3 Global,
4 Margin, 5 Monday,
6 Endear, 7 Poster, 8 Impure.
The word is: TEARDROP

247

2

248

1 D, 2 C, 3 A, 4 B, 5 E, 6 F.

249

42

250

1–D, 2–C, 3–B, 4–A, 5–E.

Solutions

251

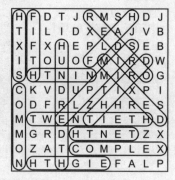

252

A – There are four different pointers appearing in turn and rotating 45 degrees clockwise. The shading is one white/two black.

253

C – A is a reflection of E and B is a reflection of D.

254

1	8	2	6	9	7	5	4	3
4	7	9	3	5	2	8	6	1
3	6	5	8	4	1	7	2	9
9	2	3	1	7	5	4	8	6
8	5	4	2	3	6	9	1	7
7	1	6	9	8	4	2	3	5
2	9	8	7	6	3	1	5	4
6	4	7	5	1	8	3	9	2
5	3	1	4	2	9	6	7	8

255

256

5

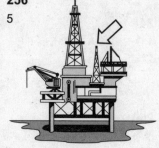

257

1 Bruckner, 2 Chicago, 3 Kansas, 4 Aloha, 5 Fail, 6 VII, 7 In, 8 D.
The character is: ROSALIND

Solutions

258

2 Ear, 3 Accra, 4 Bolivia,
5 Chauffeur, 6 Nightingale,
7 Paul McCartney.
The word is:
PACIFIC

259

260

261

1 Frill, 2 Metal, 3 April,
4 Level, 5 Model, 6 Peril,
7 Nasal, 8 Mural, 9 Growl,
10 Kneel, 11 Scowl,
12 Shell.
The word is:
REVERT

262

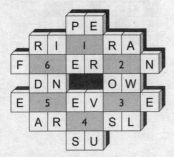

263

1 Warship, 2 Python,
3 Honest, 4 Stetson,
5 Onlooker, 6 Erode,
7 Elbow.

264

265

1 Tremor, 2 Grovel, 3 Lethal,
4 Abacus, 5 Answer,
6 Peking.
The US river is:
MOHAWK

Solutions

266

A = 4, B = 5, C = 12, D = 15,
E = 6, F = 9, G = 17, H = 27,
I = 21, J = 26, K = 44, L = 48,
M = 70, N = 92, O = 162.

267

						57
6	20	16	6	10	1	59
10	12	11	2	7	9	51
1	15	17	7	18	14	72
13	15	8	11	12	13	72
3	18	4	17	19	19	80
16	9	8	14	20	5	72
49	89	64	57	86	61	70

268

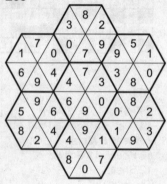

269

6	9	5	2	■	6	3	5
■	4	5	2	7	9	8	0
■	4	0	0	■	4	■	
1	2	■	3	7	8	6	1
1	■	2	8	4	3	■	2
8	3	3	■	1	■	1	3
7	2	3	4	■	4	7	4
8	0	2	■	3	7	6	6

270

2	7	6	1	8	5	9	3	4
1	4	9	2	6	3	8	7	5
3	5	8	7	9	4	6	1	2
9	2	7	4	5	1	3	8	6
8	6	4	9	3	7	2	5	1
5	1	3	8	2	6	4	9	7
6	3	1	5	4	9	7	2	8
4	8	5	3	7	2	1	6	9
7	9	2	6	1	8	5	4	3

271

E

272

B – The symbols are being
repeated, but less one
symbol in turn, i.e., spade,
diamond then heart.

Solutions

273

1 Clench, 2 Hookah, 3 Luxury,
4 Oberon, 5 Ripple, 6 Yardie.

274

$21 \times 4 + 3 - 17 = 70$

275

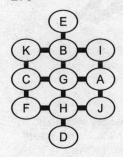

276

277

278

1 C, 2 A, 3 E, 4 B, 5 D.

279

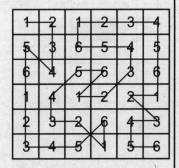

280

Please refer back to the
original puzzle and check
your answer against that.

281

B

Solutions

282

L
B
G   C

283
C

284

8	6	2	5	3	7	1	9	4
9	5	1	6	8	4	2	7	3
3	4	7	2	1	9	6	8	5
7	3	4	8	9	6	5	2	1
2	1	9	7	5	3	8	4	6
6	8	5	1	4	2	9	3	7
4	9	8	3	6	5	7	1	2
5	2	3	9	7	1	4	6	8
1	7	6	4	2	8	3	5	9

285

One possible solution is:
WIND, mind, mend, mead,
mean, MOAN

286

4S	1W	3S	3S	1W
2S	3E	3S	2W	2W
4E	1E		1N	3W
1N	3N	2E	1S	3N
3N	1N	4N	1E	3W

287

The correct definition is 3.

288

289

The nine-letter word is:
LOITERING

Solutions

290

3	4	4	2	2	4
2	1	1	1	1	2
2	1	1	1	1	2
3	2	2	3	3	3
3	2	2	3	3	3
1	3	3	4	4	2

291

The word is:
DECONTAMINATION

292

293

1 Ball, 2 East, 3 Name,
4 Face, 5 Dead, 6 Line,
7 Wool, 8 Tail.
The word is: LANCELOT

294

The colours are: CERISE,
INDIGO, MAROON,
ORANGE, PURPLE,
RUSSET, VIOLET, YELLOW.

295

The words are: BANTAM,
CANTON, DENTAL, LENTIL,
PANTRY, WINTER.

296

1 Sleeve, 2 Grainy, 3 Bantam,
4 Weight, 5 Endure, 6 Lender,
7 Wapiti, 8 Upward.
The word is: SINGULAR

297

4

298

1 A, 2 F, 3 C, 4 D, 5 E, 6 B.

299

43

300

1–C, 2–E, 3–B, 4–D, 5–A.

Solutions

301

302

C – Every alternate circle contains a small white dot. Every third circle contains a horizontal line. Every fourth circle contains a vertical line. Starting from the second circle every alternate circle contains another circle.

303

C – In all the others the figure in the middle is repeated on the outside.

304

7	1	6	2	4	8	5	3	9
8	9	5	3	1	7	2	6	4
3	2	4	5	9	6	1	8	7
1	3	7	6	2	9	4	5	8
2	4	9	1	8	5	3	7	6
5	6	8	7	3	4	9	2	1
9	5	3	8	7	1	6	4	2
4	7	2	9	6	3	8	1	5
6	8	1	4	5	2	7	9	3

305

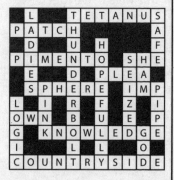

306

No 3

307

1 Minotaur, 2 Scorpio,
3 Crocus, 4 Wales, 5 Dalí,
6 Hot, 7 Me, 8 R.
The character is:
ROSSITER

Solutions

308

2 Fur, 3 Sana'a, 4 Bangkok,
5 Elizabeth, 6 Meteorology,
7 Shirley Temple.
The word is:
HUNGARY

310

312

314

309

311

1 Valet, 2 Admit, 3 Theft,
4 Audit, 5 Eight, 6 Tenet,
7 Joust, 8 Cadet, 9 Trout,
10 Scent, 11 Fleet, 12 Plait.
The word is:
DEMAND

313

1 Glacier, 2 Eruption,
3 Onset, 4 Settle, 5 Learn,
6 Nuisance, 7 Ceding.

315

1 Abused, 2 Snappy,
3 Photon, 4 Equine, 5 Terror,
6 Mentor.
The planet is:
SATURN

Solutions

316

A = 6, B = 15, C = 16,
D = 3, E = 8, F = 21, G = 31,
H = 19, I = 11, J = 52,
K = 50, L = 30, M = 102,
N = 80, O = 182.

317

						76
2	20	15	3	11	15	66
11	2	4	3	10	8	38
1	14	14	16	9	12	66
12	5	5	9	18	7	56
6	13	17	4	13	19	72
17	10	6	7	16	8	64
49	64	61	42	77	69	48

318

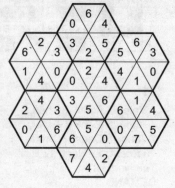

319

5	8	3	4	■	5	6	2
4	7	■	1	4	3	■	9
0	■	1	5	■	2	7	7
9	3	8	■	2	2	5	7
4	8	9	3	0	■	6	0
5	0	2	3	8	■	■	3
■	1	■	3	7	6	4	
1	7	8	9	1	3	5	■

320

2	1	6	7	9	5	8	3	4
3	5	9	1	8	4	6	2	7
8	4	7	3	6	2	1	9	5
6	3	5	9	2	1	4	7	8
4	9	2	8	5	7	3	6	1
7	8	1	4	3	6	2	5	9
5	2	4	6	1	9	7	8	3
1	6	3	5	7	8	9	4	2
9	7	8	2	4	3	5	1	6

321

A

322

D – The white dot is moving anticlockwise by 45 degrees then 90 degrees alternately.

Solutions

323

1 Agrees, 2 Despot, 3 Gyrate,
4 Jacket, 5 Masque, 6 Ribbon.

324

44 − 16 + 3 x 6 = 186

325

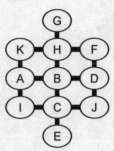

326

327

328

1 E, 2 C, 3 D, 4 B, 5 A.

329

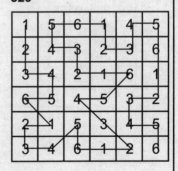

330

Please refer back to the
original puzzle and check
your answer against that.

331

F

Solutions

332

333

D

334

5	2	1	7	8	9	3	6	4
7	4	8	6	1	3	5	2	9
3	6	9	4	2	5	1	8	7
2	9	4	1	3	6	7	5	8
8	5	7	2	9	4	6	3	1
1	3	6	5	7	8	4	9	2
4	8	2	3	5	7	9	1	6
9	7	3	8	6	1	2	4	5
6	1	5	9	4	2	8	7	3

335

One possible solution is:
GRASS, grans, grins, gains,
pains, pawns, LAWNS

336

3S	3E	1W	4S	1W
1E	2E	2E	1W	2S
1N	2E		1E	4W
3E	1S	3N	1W	1S
4N	2N	2N	1W	4W

337

The correct definition is 2.

338

339

The nine-letter word is:
SPACEWALK

Solutions

340

2	3	3	2	2	1
2	4	4	1	1	4
2	4	4	1	1	4
2	1	1	3	3	4
2	1	1	3	3	4
1	1	1	4	4	1

341

The word is:
DISENFRANCHISED

342

343

1 Hand, 2 Lime, 3 Bush,
4 Cart, 5 Open, 6 Ever,
7 Step, 8 Fair.
The word is: DISCOVER

344

The minerals, metals
and gems are: COPPER,
GALENA, GARNET,
GYPSUM, JASPER,
RADIUM, SILVER, ZIRCON.

345

The words are: CRITIC,
EDITOR, GLITCH, GUITAR,
LOITER, WRITHE.

346

1 Morsel, 2 Button, 3 Custom,
4 Menial, 5 Maiden, 6 Chapel,
7 Guitar, 8 Larynx.
The word is: ROSEMARY

347

7

348

1 B, 2 D, 3 A, 4 E, 5 C, 6 F.

349

87

350

1–A, 2–D, 3–C, 4–E, 5–B.

Solutions

351

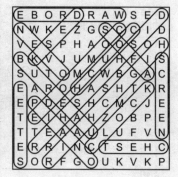

352

D – A white dot is added below the others at each stage. Once added, dots change from white to black, and vice versa, at each stage.

353

E – The others are all the same figure rotated. E is a reflection of the other figures, not a rotation.

354

5	6	1	2	4	9	7	8	3
4	7	9	3	1	8	5	6	2
3	2	8	6	5	7	1	9	4
7	4	2	9	6	5	3	1	8
8	1	3	4	7	2	6	5	9
9	5	6	1	8	3	2	4	7
6	8	5	7	2	4	9	3	1
2	9	4	5	3	1	8	7	6
1	3	7	8	9	6	4	2	5

355

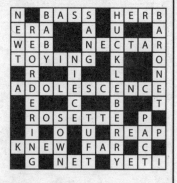

356

6

357

1 Kasparov, 2 Tbilisi, 3 Apollo, 4 April, 5 Cage, 6 Tin, 7 It, 8 A.
The character is: VIOLENTA

Solutions

358

2 Dog, 3 Kenya, 4 Moldova,
5 Hudson Bay, 6 Kuala
Lumpur, 7 Bactrian camel.
The word is:
GONDOLA

360

362

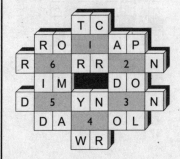

364

359

361

1 Often, 2 Bacon, 3 Nylon,
4 Green, 5 Arson, 6 Baron,
7 Stern, 8 Grain, 9 Raven,
10 Heron, 11 Plain,
12 Ocean.
The word is:
CAREER

363

1 Mercury, 2 Yield, 3 Drama,
4 Malaria, 5 Avoid, 6 Idealist,
7 Storm.

365

1 Legend, 2 Saloon,
3 Phobia, 4 Acetic, 5 Ferric,
6 Wither.
The famous Rocky
Mountains peak is: ELBERT

Solutions

366

A = 5, B = 16, C = 13, D = 4,
E = 18, F = 21, G = 29,
H = 17, I = 22, J = 50,
K = 46, L = 39, M = 96,
N = 85, O = 181.

368

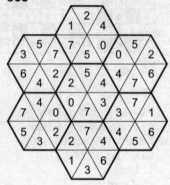

367

							62
18	7	18	19	4	10	76	
17	13	9	3	1	5	48	
5	8	20	19	2	15	69	
2	4	16	6	11	6	45	
9	3	12	12	20	10	66	
13	11	7	1	8	14	54	
64	46	82	60	46	60	91	

369

3	1	8			9	7	6
7		2	7	2	4		5
6	1	9	7		3		6
	0		1	1	5	9	8
2		4	7	9	7	4	
3	5	4		9		4	5
9	3		7		8	0	7
	2	2	3	5	5	9	

370

4	6	8	2	5	9	1	3	7
9	3	2	1	7	4	8	6	5
5	1	7	3	8	6	2	9	4
8	9	1	6	4	2	7	5	3
2	5	6	9	3	7	4	1	8
7	4	3	8	1	5	6	2	9
1	8	9	7	2	3	5	4	6
6	7	4	5	9	1	3	8	2
3	2	5	4	6	8	9	7	1

371

C

372

B – Each of the three triangles
rotates 180 degrees.

Solutions

373

1 Italic, 2 Mature, 3 Plural,
4 Tehran, 5 Vulgar, 6 Zodiac.

374

66 + 22 − 41 x 5 = 235

375

◆	■	□	♎	⌘
□	♎	⌘	◆	■
♎	⌘	◆	■	□
■	□	♎	⌘	◆
⌘	◆	■	□	♎

376

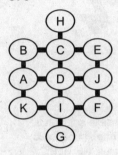

377

378

1 A, 2 B, 3 D, 4 E, 5 C.

379

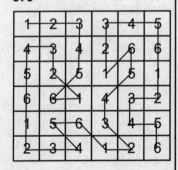

380

Please refer back to the
original puzzle and check
your answer against that.

381

H

Solutions

382

383

F

384

3	7	6	4	8	2	5	1	9
8	4	5	9	7	1	2	3	6
2	1	9	6	3	5	7	8	4
9	2	7	1	5	3	4	6	8
5	3	4	8	2	6	1	9	7
1	6	8	7	4	9	3	2	5
4	5	3	2	9	8	6	7	1
7	9	1	3	6	4	8	5	2
6	8	2	5	1	7	9	4	3

385

One possible solution is:
ROOF, hoof, hood, hold,
told, toll, till, TILE

386

4E	2S	3S	2S	2W
2S	2E	3S	3W	2W
2E	1N		3W	1N
3N	3E	1E	3N	1N
1E	4N	2E	3W	1W

387

The correct definition is 3.

388

389

The nine-letter word is:
KNOWLEDGE

476

Solutions

390

1	1	1	2	2	3
2	2	2	3	3	1
2	2	2	3	3	1
1	4	4	3	3	1
1	4	4	3	3	1
1	3	3	2	2	1

391

The word is:
COUNTERMEASURES

392

393

1 Book, 2 Hand or Paid,
3 Pole, 4 Cape, 5 Hare,
6 Race, 7 Bear, 8 Wind.
The word is: KALAHARI

394

The buildings are: CASTLE,
CHURCH, MOSQUE,
MUSEUM, PAGODA,
PALACE, SCHOOL,
TEMPLE.

395

The words are: ANNOYS,
CANOPY, DENOTE, GENOME,
IGNORE, RENOWN.

396

1 Dragon, 2 Maniac, 3 Ritual,
4 Thread, 5 Action, 6 Anchor,
7 Kidnap, 8 Plural.
The word is: NAUTICAL

397

1. 4
2. 2
3. 3

398

1 C, 2 E, 3 B, 4 F, 5 A, 6 D.

399

62

400

1–A, 2–E, 3–D, 4–C, 5–B.

Solutions

401

402

B – At each stage the figure rotates 45 degrees.

403

D – It spirals anticlockwise from outside to inside. The others spiral clockwise from the outside.

404

6	1	5	7	3	2	8	4	9
2	8	9	6	1	4	7	5	3
3	7	4	5	8	9	6	1	2
4	9	8	2	5	3	1	6	7
7	2	3	1	4	6	5	9	8
5	6	1	9	7	8	2	3	4
1	4	2	3	6	7	9	8	5
9	3	6	8	2	5	4	7	1
8	5	7	4	9	1	3	2	6

405

406

4 – A leaf on the stalk to the right of the middle has moved up.

407

1 Khartoum, 2 Albania, 3 Boxing, 4 Below, 5 *Taxi*, 6 Cat, 7 DC, 8 H.
The character is: MAGWITCH

Solutions

408

2 Ark, 3 Seine, 4 Myanmar, 5 Anchorage, 6 Arctic Ocean, 7 Campanologist. The word is: ORINOCO

410

412

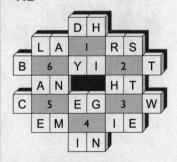

414

409

411

1 Given, 2 Drain, 3 Pecan, 4 Dozen, 5 Pagan, 6 Blown, 7 Align, 8 Human, 9 Drown, 10 Canon, 11 Linen, 12 Prawn. The word is: AMAZON

413

1 Atheist, 2 Status, 3 Useful, 4 Ultimate, 5 Teddy, 6 Dynamite, 7 Terra.

415

1 Mallet, 2 Reagan, 3 Walrus, 4 Poetry, 5 Exodus, 6 Shoddy. The city is: LAREDO

Solutions

416

A = 3, B = 14, C = 7, D = 1,
E = 12, F = 17, G = 21,
H = 8, I = 13, J = 38, K = 29,
L = 21, M = 67, N = 50,
O = 117.

418

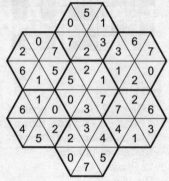

417

							62
14	19	20	15	6	16	90
8	5	18	4	12	17	64
11	17	13	2	19	7	69
1	4	18	7	20	16	66
1	9	10	3	8	6	37
5	2	14	3	15	9	48
40	56	93	34	80	71	56

419

1	5	2	5	9	■	4	
5	■	8	4	■	3	1	2
3	5	■	4	9	2	1	8
7	3	■	2	■	1	■	5
■	1	■	2	3	9	2	1
5	9	■	■	9	0	■	2
9	■	7	7	5	■	6	6
4	8	4	8	■	3	3	3

421

A

422

D – The white dot moves one corner clockwise at each stage, the black dot moves from left to right at the bottom and the line alternates between two sets of corners.

420

4	1	2	7	3	8	6	9	5
5	3	7	4	6	9	8	2	1
8	9	6	2	5	1	4	3	7
6	2	4	8	9	7	1	5	3
9	8	5	3	1	6	7	4	2
3	7	1	5	2	4	9	6	8
2	6	8	9	7	5	3	1	4
7	5	9	1	4	3	2	8	6
1	4	3	6	8	2	5	7	9